EXCUSE ME, DOCTOR

Frederick Stacey

Copyright © 2023 Frederick Stacey

All rights reserved

No part of this book may be reproduced, or stored in a retrieval system, or transmitted in any form or by any means, electronic, mechanical, photocopying, recording, or otherwise, without express written permission of the publisher.

I'd like to thank my wife Susie for her support and encouragement to write this memoir

To the those staff of the NHS that were lost during the global pandemic

To all my colleagues past and present, thankyou for the good times

EXCUSE ME, DOCTOR

Frederick Stacey

1

 I am not a doctor, nor have I ever been to medical school. The reason for the title of this book will become apparent later.
When I left school in nineteen seventy-seven, I wasn't your academic heading for university or even further education, I was for a more practical hands-on approach to earning a living. Throughout my later schooling I had a notion that I wanted to be a television cameraman for the BBC. Thinking back, I realise that my whole approach to getting involved was more akin to Yosser Hughes from the TV series Boys from the Black Stuff, "I can do that. Gissa job". Perhaps not quite that bad but I had no qualifications and no experience in the field and no real idea of what I needed to do to get there. I left school with a handful of CSE's (Certificate of Secondary Education) that, as it turned out was a complete waste of time as nobody was interested in them. If you didn't have O levels also known as GCE's that was it. So, after several attempts and the receiving of several cards with "The engineering recruitment officer regrets to inform you that blah blah blah" I resigned myself to the fact that it wasn't going to happen. As it turned out I wouldn't have made it anyway as I am colourblind and normal colour vision was one of the prerequisites. I did in the future, as a member of The Ermine Street Guard take part in several BBC programs and on my own as a supporting artiste in Casualty and Doctor Who.
Once I'd left school, I decided that perhaps a career in the RAF

might be a good option as I have an interest in helicopters and flight in general. No chance, after passing various aptitude tests I was sent for a medical, normal colour vision was needed there too. The same for the Royal Navy.

So, what could I do? I went to the job centre and got sent (that's how it worked in those days) to an electrical appliance warehouse that had a vacancy. I turned up spoke to the manager and started work as a warehouseman the next day. I was now an employed person and I have to say that while warehouse work was physical it was quite enjoyable. I worked for them for a while before they went to the wall and I found myself unemployed again,

I can't remember for how long I was out of permanent employment as I took on temporary work including a short stint at Tesco, every little helps. Then I spotted a small ad in the classified section of the local paper, Trainee Sound and Lighting Technician wanted, Stardust Cabaret Club, Usk, I was straight on the phone. The Stardust was a popular entertainment venue throughout the sixties and seventies with some high-profile acts appearing there.

I went for an "interview" one Sunday evening and was taken into the club where we all sat around a large table. I answered their questions to the best of my ability, and they agreed a trial period of I think was a month. While we sat at the table Chris Parfitt who was the head of the sound and lighting department pointed to the table next to us and said, "This next week we've got these pair of clowns performing." I looked to the other table where Sid Little and Eddie Large, a very famous comedy double act of the late nineteen seventies, was sat having a drink.

I started as a trainee in the sound and lighting department and to this day state that it was the best job I'd ever had. The pay wasn't great, but the job satisfaction was immense. It was like a party every night, actually, there was a party every night, so no wonder I liked the job. I met and worked (and partied) with some of the UK's top entertainers of the day. The first was the aforementioned Little and Large which was a great experience. I worked with a host of famous and not so famous people including Des O'Connor,

Roger De Courcey (and of course, Nookie the Bear) Danny La Rue and Paul Daniels. Bernard Manning had a "stag night" there with three strippers which, for a spotty faced eighteen-year-old was an experience to say the least.

I was in the sound box sorting stuff out for that nights show when in walked a woman in a loose-fitting top. "Hello" she said. I was an innocent and naïve eighteen-year-old (I know, nothing's changed apart from the age). "Hello" I replied nervously. The club band were on stage rehearsing, and I was looking after the sound desk. As we watched and chatted, she leaned on my shoulder. I didn't know what to do, so I just stared straight ahead with the occasional glance to this older woman. She chatted to me about the work (mine, not hers) then she gave me a cassette with her "performance" music on it and went off to the dressing room (never has a title been more appropriate). When I looked at the tape, I noticed that it was partly run on, so I went down to the dressing room to check it was at the right place. Backstage there were three dressing rooms, two small rooms and one larger one with a star on the door for the main act. The woman was in one of the smaller rooms. I knocked on the door and a voice shouted "Come in" so in I went. I entered and the woman was stood just out of sight behind the door, as I turned towards her, I stood frozen to the spot not knowing where to look. She was completely stark naked. I stutteringly (remember I was only eighteen and quite shy) explained that the tape was partly run on whilst I looked in every direction bar at her. At that moment Nigel, (I had no idea what his job was, I wasn't even sure if he was employed there or was just one of the owner's friends), walked past the door and immediately jumped to the wrong conclusion. He saw me later and gave a wink while tapping his nose. Pointless to protest and on reflection it didn't do my reputation any harm. Anyway, the show went on with the three strippers getting their kit off and Bernard Manning being his usual blue self.

 TV's Opportunity Knocks winner Tammy Jones was appearing the week after we'd played host to the Three Degrees. The trio wanted a particular colour gel to go on a spotlight at the back of the stage which when lit spread a pink glow around the edge of the singers. As the gel was expensive, we left it in situ for use again.

Tammy stood on the stage singing Let Me Try Again, her big hit and as it was a big number with her raising her arms at the finale of the song, we decided to fade up the pink light. The audience must have thought it was amazing as the light shone straight through her dress like she was having an x ray. You could almost see everything underneath, almost.

I had a fantastic few years working at the Stardust Club with loads more stories to be told another time, meeting and partying with celebs but eventually, they closed "for refurbishment". The cabaret circuit at that stage was on the decline so it was only a matter of time before it closed. They promised that they would be open again in three weeks. Three weeks came and went, and I needed to know if I was going to be employed again. Time went on but I needed money. So off I went to the job centre again and emerged with more temporary warehouse work. This warehouse was the UK distribution centre for MB Games, a manufacturer of some of the most popular board games and toys. I was taken on for six months leading up to Christmas which was useful as I had a discount on some of the products. I worked for them the following year, again for another six months and was in line for a permanent job but due to a problem with one of the chargehands that ended in a court case (he had light fingers) and me as witness for the prosecution I never went back. If I had got the permanent job this would be a very different memoir. So yet again I was out of work. My dad was self-employed so for a time I helped with his work which gave me few quid.

My best friend Steve Pullen's brother-in-law Mike Gwillym was Deputy Head porter at the Royal Gwent Hospital and told me about a porter's job that was going. He told me to turn up that afternoon and see the Head Porter, Bryn Davies for an informal interview. Bryn took one look at me and said, "I like the fact that you wore a tie, not many do". After a few questions and descriptions of what the job entailed (he said, "People die, how do you feel about dealing with dead bodies?" My first day in the job entailed such a scenario). I was a bit apprehensive about this task, but I needed to work so would cross that bridge when I came to it. Eventually he said that I could have the job, he just needed to speak to the powers that be. I went home and hadn't been in the house long when the phone rang. I could start the next day.

That was my entrance into thirty-eight years in the NHS. February nineteen eighty-three saw me start as a general porter then becoming a blood / pathology porter following that twelve years later I moved up to endoscopy as an assistant eventually becoming senior assistant with responsibility for training junior assistants amongst other things. A further twelve years later in two thousand and five I applied for and got a job as trainee Clinical Technologist in a cancer hospital in Cardiff, then eventually in twenty nineteen getting a senior post, the job required a science qualification to be eligible for the Register of Clinical Technologists so in two thousand and five off I went all be it apprehensively, to university in my late forties. That was an experience that I'll go into later.

2

My first day as a porter went well with my very first job being to remove a body from the ward to the mortuary. To be fair, the guys in the porter's room said I didn't need to go as it was my first day but as I stated to them "I'll have to do it sometime" so off I went with Harry Goulding, a seasoned porter of many years' experience whose daughter was a radiographer in the same hospital. We did the job and went back to the porter's room where I was properly introduced to the rest of the crew, I worked with these guys for twelve years and had an absolute blast. Sad to say a few of them have passed on, and at a relatively young age. I will say though that in my mind's eye I still see them as they were. When I meet them it's quite a shock to see how they've aged, I suppose that works both ways.

When I first went to work at the hospital I started as a day porter which I did for a while. I moved to continental shifts which I liked as it gave time off during the week. I applied for a job as a blood porter also on a rotating shift pattern because the money was better, and it suited me. My first day as blood porter I was shown the ropes by Norman Chapman, another blood porter. He took to me the pathology laboratories and introduced me to the staff there. One such introduction was to Ronny (Veronica) Greenfield who worked in the blood bank and became my wife in nineteen eighty-five. We had a daughter, Joanne in nineteen eighty-seven. We divorced in nineteen ninety-eight.

The only shift I wasn't too fussed on was afternoons, two until ten o'clock because you couldn't do much that day because you were waiting to go to work, and it was too late to do anything when you got home. Anyway, as I became more experienced it became easier and we had some great laughs along the way.

Going back to Bryn Davies saying he liked that I wore a tie for the interview, they interviewed for more porters a little while after I'd been employed there, and one turned up in his best bib and tucker. After the interview he'd got the job and could start the next day. The following morning, he turned up hair all spiked up and chains from his ears and a spiked leather belt. He was a bit of a nutter as it turned out, but it amused us, the rest of the porters no end. He was sent home and told to return in more appropriate clothing.

In the blood bank on nights

A change of uniform

I'm a little unclear about some of my progression through the porter's department because I did work in the general pool and did overtime in other departments. Thirty-eight plus years has made some of it a bit hazy. I worked in all the porter's departments at some time as overtime or holiday cover, so these were little asides from my main employment. Talking of which I volunteered to do a few overtime shifts as gynae theatre porter. The job entailed ferrying patients from the wards to theatres and back again, sorting theatre waste and general tasks as directed by the theatre Sister. I was waiting for a procedure to finish and was chatting to the sister. She asked, "Have you ever seen an operation?" To which I replied that I hadn't. "Put a cap and mask on and go and have a look" she said. I thought she was taking the mick at first, but she insisted. So, I donned the theatre attire and went into the operating theatre expecting to be bollocked by the surgeon. The surgeon was at the table removing a cyst from a woman's abdomen that was the size of a small football. I really don't know how but I ended up stood at the table directly opposite the surgeon watching in graphic detail the removal of the cyst whilst having a running commentary on what was going on. When I had to leave, he nodded to me, and I replied "Thank you" as I turned towards the door. It turned out that he thought I was a medical student hence the commentary, fascinating to say the least. It was like a scene from the film Paper Mask, where a hospital porter assumes the identity of a newly qualified doctor that was killed in a car accident. Anyway, I digress. My wife Sue a nurse, was appalled when she read that the sister had let me go into theatre to watch. Different times when GDPR didn't exist.

On nightshifts, once the main work was done, and if it was quiet, at about one to two in the morning we'd settle down in the porter's room and get some sleep, answering any calls that came in. Usually, it was changing Entonox cylinders on the labour ward or removing a body to the mortuary, sometimes collecting notes from the ante natal clinic for the maternity ward.

The collecting of notes was a somewhat spooky job; the ante natal clinic was a separate building from the main hospital with a link corridor for access. The building was constructed in the nineteen sixties and the notes were stored in the basement of this building which was quiet and dark in the middle of the night. You'd unlock the doors and make your way to the staircase in the middle of the clinic and descend into the darkness. Unlock the door to the basement and enter, switch on the light which wasn't particularly bright and walk through all the racks of notes which were, naturally, in alphabetical order with only a narrow gap between the racks. After several visits you tended to note where each letter of the alphabet started and ended so you could be in and out quickly. Fumbling in the semi darkness you would hear clicks and clacks from the racking and odd noises coming from dark corners. Once you'd retrieved the notes you would reverse the entry process and get out as quickly as possible. At the link corridor invariably one of the porters would hide behind a door and as you walked out would just say "Hiya" to which the notes would fly in the air followed by a few expletives, well actually, a lot of expletives.

While I'm on the subject about collecting notes, we used to on occasions in the middle of the night, have to collect notes from medical records in the outpatient's department. This was a very large hall in the old part of the hospital. To get to it you'd have to unlock a door that led down some stairs to an access corridor underneath the paediatric ward. This corridor had tunnels leading off that were in complete darkness and even for someone who is not of nervous disposition like me it could be a very spooky experience. These tunnels housed the pathology department in days of old and a rumour had it that a biochemist took his own life in one of the tunnels further adding to the spooky atmosphere. I myself thought it was an urban myth, but it was retold by different people at different times, so you never know. You could hear the floorboards above creaking as people moved overhead. When you unlocked the door to the outpatient's hall there was a lot of creaking and groaning and echoing in the hall as the racks of notes settled, sometimes a draught would whistle through making the hairs stand up on the back of your neck. As with the antenatal clinic you'd memorise where the notes were and exited as quickly as possible.

Block with the Ante Natal Clinic to the front

One of the jobs that we were often called for in the middle of the night was to change the Entonox cylinder on labour ward. This entailed going through a door on level two, into the ducts and out the back of the hospital across the back road to the oxy bank as it was called. The ducts (service tunnels under the hospital where a lot of pipework was situated) were, naturally, in darkness. You'd open the door to be greeted by scuttling sounds and you could sense that something was there. The light switch was, unfortunately situated behind the door so you had to fumble in the darkness to find it. As soon as the light came on you would see the source of the scuttling. Cockroaches, hundreds of them some with antennae so long they could pick up BBC One. Fortunately, if you waited a couple of seconds, they would all disappear into their respective hideaways. On more than one occasion I fumbled for the switch only to catch hold of a monster cockroach. Before I learned to switch on the light, I would just walk through to the sound of crunch, crunch, crunch.

In later years while on nights we'd explore some of the ducts underneath the old Victorian part of the hospital as there was an entrance directly under the porter's room. Block C of the hospital had been built behind the old block, when you went into the tunnels in some parts, you'd come up against a dead end full of rubble where they just bulldozed the old buildings. The main tunnel followed the main corridor and that in turn went off towards Belle View Lane and another tunnel leading up to St Woolos Hospital an even older building that was the former workhouse situated at the top of Stow Hill in Newport. This carried things like telephone cables and the like and became quite narrow as it went up the hill towards the other hospital.

I used to enjoy exploring the old tunnels, but you could always guarantee that as soon I was "underground" my pager would go off and I'd have to find my way back usually alone and in the dark because the others would have the torch.

I recall one night I didn't go with the boys as I was quite busy. Billy Saville, Gary May and Phil Rogers, who was the chargehand were down in the tunnel while I was in the main corridor above them. Someone, I can't remember who, I think it was a maintenance person, came up to me asking if I knew where Phil was. I pointed to the ground whereupon you could hear the three of them talking to each other as they walked beneath us. I did get a funny look until I explained their exploration antics.

Porter's room bottom right with entrance to the tunnels below the windows. Octagonal building is ENT theatre, temp buildings housed the hospital chapel.

There were quite a few porters on different shifts plus quite a few day porters in the general pool One such porter bore a striking resemblance to Saddam Hussein the disgraced and eventually executed Iraqi dictator, much to his annoyance and as you can imagine in the days when you could say things to people whether it upset them or not, the boys would make the most of it. One day he brought a small decorative plate into the room with a view to it brightening up the place. On one wall was a blackboard and to the left was a small hook to which he hung the plate. It was an unusual decoration for a porter's room but there you go; woe betide anyone who touched it. One night shift I took the plate down and drew with a China graph pencil a crack on the front and around the back. I placed it back on the wall and from a short distance it really looked like it had been damaged. He was due in for the morning shift so we waited to see what he would do. At six in the morning, he and his mates made their appearance. He put his things in his locker and put the kettle on and sat at the table. With that he stood up ranting about people not looking after things as he stamped towards the plate. As you can imagine, we were in fits of laughter as he went on and on. Eventually I took the plate from him and wiped away the marks. I think at that point he cast a doubt on my parentage. He did see the funny side eventually. I tried that trick on a few others with their drinking cups with varying degrees of success.

In the good old days, we would receive our pay weekly with the wage coming in small brown envelopes. You'd go to a hatch at the general office and receive your packet. One porter used to have to hand over his envelope to his wife who would take out the contents and give him his "cut". She did this to prevent him squandering his wages in the bookies. To get round this he would slide a pencil into the top of the packet and rotate it several times and then withdraw the pencil. This would then have a tenner, or a fiver and sometimes twenty-pound note wrapped around it. He did this for quite a while until she caught on to his ploy. It turned out that this technique was used fraudulently so they started putting a staple through the packet preventing any removal of cash much to his annoyance. Monthly payments straight into the bank didn't come in for some time later so receiving a little brown packet was how the wages were distributed. Security was an issue as a large amount of money was brought into the hospital via a security guard.

3

I was walking around the outside of the hospital towards the casualty department one daytime when I could see a few people had gathered, staring up at a window at the top of the casualty porter's room. When I got there, I could see Phil Taylor crouched on top of the lockers, he was totally unaware of the crowd that had gathered to see what he was doing. It turned out his mate had popped out and Phil decided he would spring a surprise on him upon his return. It didn't happen, Phil turned his head towards us and realised he looked a right chump on top of the lockers so abandoned his surprise. These are the sort of things that we (the porters) and others got up to when there were quiet periods. These little acts of larking about fizzled out eventually and as I say to this day, all the fun has been taken out of the NHS. I don't mean being frivolous is acceptable but given the nature of the work and some of the things that are seen and must be dealt with, a little bit of frivolity helps to let off steam and maintains morale and everyone knows that people in the health service have a dark sense of humour.
The casualty department as did other departments in the hospital have their own dedicated teams of porters covering all the shifts giving a twenty-four-hour service. When I was a blood porter, I could wander the hospital at will and base myself anywhere as

long as I was near a phone. Casualty (now called ER or A and E) was an interesting base because one, a lot of my work came from that department and two, I was on occasions asked to help by fetching and carrying or some other simple tasks. I would sometimes sit in the porter's room and have a cuppa with the boys. Two such guys were Jim Livingstone a Londoner from Fulham and Doug Truman. Jim was a smoker (you could smoke almost anywhere in those days) who smoked roll ups. The thing about roll ups is they keep going out, so Jim was constantly lighting his fag, shaking the match and tossing it into the bin next to him which was just a yellow plastic bag held on a frame. Doug had just made a pot of tea and was letting it brew when Jim exclaimed in his cockney accent while tugging at his collar, "It's fucking hot in here" to which I looked up to see the bin fully ablaze. Jim stood up with a few more expletives grabbed Doug's pot of tea and tipped the lot onto the fire. Doug was not amused. I was doubled up laughing at the scene happening before me. It wouldn't have looked out of place on a TV comedy show. Jim passed away a few years later and a few of us made the trip up to Fulham for his funeral.

At one time on a night shift, Doug had a radio in the room and couldn't get it to tune in, he knew I was technically minded and asked if I could look at it. I took it to the main porter's room where I had tools in my locker. Once I'd dismantled the radio, I could see that the string that was wound around the tuning section had come off. These are an absolute nightmare to put back on and can be near impossible without a specific diagram. The only way I could get it to work was to make two small holes in the side of the radio and attach the cord to the tuner and pass the cord through the holes. To tune the radio, you had to pull either the top cord or the bottom cord to move the dial one way or the other. Phil Rogers who'd been watching me fix it followed me down to the casualty porters' room and stood outside as I explained to Doug that to tune the radio, he'd have to pull the cords and he could only get two or three stations on it. He was looking at me as if I'd just dropped out of the sky while saying "That's great, as long as it works" I left him to it and went with Phil back to the main porter's room laughing all the way.

I had a bit of a reputation for being a gadget man (still do as it happens). Stefan Senese gave me the nickname Inspector Gadget and whenever I did anything that entailed the use of something technical, they would start "singing" the James Bond theme. Then my nickname changed to Bond. Fred Bond.

Some afternoons I'd bring my Commodore 64 home computer into work, and we'd borrow a telly from one of the wards usually A1 East. We'd all be gathered around the computer, playing role playing adventure games to pass the time between jobs. This became a bit of a pastime with our shift, and we'd all be there trying to work out the cryptic clues. If a job came in we would stop and wait until everyone was back in the room. I bought a speech synthesiser module for it and we had hours of fun making it say swear words or complete sentences with expletives throughout. It was quite amusing listening to this robotic voice cussing and swearing, saying everything phonetically– simple pleasures, or simple porters!

There was a porter who worked permanent nights. He worked at the hospital for very many years and wore a brown full length porters coat, straight out of the fifties and sixties. It was rumoured that they'd built the hospital around him and that he was one of the fixtures and fittings. He wasn't a people person and when he came in to work, he would put on his brown coat, take his boots off and plonk himself into a large chair in the corner of the room, read his paper and go to sleep later in the night. He did the odd job when it came in but really didn't do a lot. If you tried to speak or pass the time of day with him, he would just grunt or ignore you or sometimes tell you to go forth and multiply.

Every night after he'd gone to sleep his false teeth would slowly slide out of his mouth eventually coming right out and landing with a crash on the floor. He would wake up, retrieve his teeth and promptly put them back in his mouth, fluff and all.

One such time the teeth were making their way out of his mouth, and we were all waiting for the crash. The teeth made a bid for freedom, shooting slightly up into the air, but there was no crash. Consequently, he wasn't woken up and carried on snoring ignorant that his teeth had escaped. A quick look over by his chair revealed that they had taken refuge in his boots. When the time came to prepare to go home, they were retrieved and replaced back into captivity. While talking about this character has reminded me of a practical joke we played on him. We were all sat around the table playing cards or reading papers and drinking tea (what a life). He settled into his chair and promptly went to sleep. We'd concocted a plan that about two o'clock in the morning very quietly we'd get our coats on and get ourselves ready as if we were going home. Once we were all ready, we switched on the lights and started making noises and opening our lockers as if we were going. At the appointed time, the lights went on and suddenly he hurriedly jumped-up rushing to put his boots on as he'd thought he'd overslept. We were roaring laughing as we all settled down again to the rail of four-letter abuse coming from him. We didn't care as there was no love lost between us.

Talking of working nights, it was a strange experience eating your main meal at about one or two in the morning. We never gave a second thought at eating lasagne and chips at that late hour, it's a wonder I'm not the size of a house, it must be my genes.

In the nineteen-eighties the canteen offered a twenty-four-hour service with hot meals being served until about two or three in the morning. When I first started, there was a catering assistant who would give us our food and not take any money for it. Of course, being low paid porters, we accepted her generosity. Eventually, after several years she was "let go" but by then the canteen was closing at around midnight and food was obtained via a vending machine. Years later the canteen was modernised into a dining room with soup and salad islands and a new hot service area but closed in the evenings.

The canteen in the 1980's

The canteen in the 1990's

In the "old" canteen there was a coffee lounge just off to the side that became a smoking area when it was outlawed in the main dining area. Eventually a room was designated for smokers next to of all places the anaesthetics department. I had to go and get someone from there once and on opening the door the stink was horrendous and the smoke was so thick you couldn't see anyone in the room. Eventually a long time after, smoking was banned from inside the building followed sometime later by a complete ban on all hospital premises.

Talking of the canteen facilities, opposite the main canteen was a satellite dining room specifically for consultants only. Eventually this was closed and converted for use by the radiology department as the gamma camera suite. I can remember at that time nobody had heard of Nuclear Medicine. It caused a bit of a stir when the sign went up that said Gamma Camera Suite. I will go into my Nuclear Medicine exploits later in the book.

4

In nineteen eighty-six I had a call from the casualty department whilst on the night shift. In the early hours of the morning my pager went off and when I phoned back Sister Theresa Sheridan said, "Can you come down to resus". I thought it unusual as normally they would ask me to take a blood sample or similar. Off I went and entered resus via the plastic flap doors. "Is this your dad?" Sister Sheridan asked showing me an admission sheet. "Yes" I replied, "where is he?". She pointed to the resus rooms so in I went. My dad was on a trolley, he was sort of with it but clearly, he'd had a stroke, he couldn't speak, and I could tell he was frightened and frustrated. Eventually he was admitted to A1 East, the acute admission ward. From there he went to A2 East where he stayed for a few days. The ward sister, Sue Barker (more on her later) informed us that my dad was to be moved to Rowan Ward, a stroke unit at County Hospital near Pontypool. This would prove to be awkward for my mother to visit him as she would have to rely on family to drive her there. I rode a motorcycle at that time so visited as often as I could.

Dad languished in that ward for eight months before passing away. I don't think he had the best care there as I'd go into his room, and he'd look at me and would be chewing on his blanket. He was hungry. I went there one day and there was a small bowl of cold food on the table. It appeared they had brought the food in left it and came back in a while and took it away again. He'd had a stroke so couldn't feed himself. I did take some biscuits and soft food in for him, but it was difficult to get him to eat it. We had a few calls in the middle of the night over a few weeks to say we should come to the ward as he may not last the night. Each time he'd rally so we'd go back home. One night the phone rang. It was the ward Sister to inform us that my dad had passed away.

I was married to Ronny at this time, and she was pregnant with our daughter Joanne. I managed to tell my dad of the pregnancy, but I don't know if he understood or not. It's my one regret that he never got to see my daughter – the only grandchild he didn't meet. When it came to compassionate leave, I was given just one day. I think you get a bit more these days as one day just wasn't enough to do things like register the death and attend the funeral for which I think I booked annual leave.

My Dad

5

It's interesting to recall how health and safety (or the lack of it) was dealt with back in the day. Near the porter's room in the centre of block A, the original part of the hospital, was a service lift that went the entire four floors of the block, the other public lifts only went to three. The top floor in the centre of block A was for a time doctor's residences, I can't remember what was on the next floor down, I have vague notion it was nursing administration, but I can't be sure. The first floor housed the coronary care unit and below that was the main entrance with a few offices leading off. In the early days of the hospital the main entrance was reserved for consultants and bigwigs only, woe betide the mere mortals if they decided to use it. The side entrance was for the rank and file of the hospital.

This service lift was an old wooden walled affair with a concertina cage door and a metal folding outer door. If the lift was at the top, the doors could still be opened with a small drop onto the buffers which consisted of large springs. Billy Saville and Glyn

Davies were going on a job and were taking the service lift. Billy pulled open the door and could see that the lift wasn't there, it was very dark in the lift shaft and the light was quite dim in that part of the corridor. He stepped off the side and dropped into the buffer zone which was about four feet below. As he did, he screamed as if he dropped a very long way. Glyn ran to the door screaming "Billy, Billy". Of course, Billy was unharmed and stood up crying laughing. At least he knew Glyn cared. But the fact that you could open the doors when the lift wasn't there was certainly a health and safety issue and luckily nobody else had used the lift otherwise Billy might have been squished.

There were another two lifts that could be opened when the lift wasn't there, one was in the main corridor by A1 East the other by the fracture and orthopaedic clinic. When the old hospital was being demolished, I took the manufacturer's plaque off the one by A1 East which is now screwed to my shed door, it seems a lifetime away since I was there.

Another porter in our crew was the ever-popular Norman Chapman who would have everybody in stitches with his antics. I liked working with Norman because he was so entertaining. My stomach would hurt by the end of the shift for all the laughing. Norman was a confirmed bachelor who lived with his mother and a half a dozen or so cats, he acted as carer for his mother. He rode an old-fashioned pushbike everywhere including when shopping, putting the carrier bags onto the handlebars. I found a similar machine in my parent's shed and after replacing brakes and tyres used it for a time as transport back and forth to work. Norman's bike didn't have effective brakes, so he used to jump off and run alongside until it stopped. A year or so later I decided to purchase a modern bicycle, so I gave my old bike to Norman. He was so appreciative and used that bike for very many years. Unfortunately, my new bike was stolen so I was consigned to walking back and forth to work again which didn't do my fitness any harm.

One time it was drizzling as I plodded home and I was tired. As I walked past Ken Roberts Motorcycles on Caerleon Road in

Newport in the window was a gleaming sporty looking Suzuki. In I went, had a sit on it, took a brochure and decided there and then I was going to be a motorcyclist. I took the brochure home and showed it to Ronny. I rode this bike everywhere and loved it until one February lunchtime in nineteen eighty-nine just after I'd finished work.

I was riding home after a morning shift and had stopped at traffic lights outside the former Odeon cinema, now known as the Neon in Clarence Place. The lights changed and the cars in front all set off with me behind. As we were passing the tax offices in Clarence Place, Newport the traffic unusually, came to a halt. Unfortunately, I was looking behind me and when I'd turned around again went straight into the back of a Ford Granada. I was catapulted into the back windscreen and fell off into the middle of the road, I was lucky not to have been hit or run over by the traffic on the opposite side. Once I'd gathered my senses, I looked up to see all the windows in the tax offices full of people staring down at the scene below. A crowd had gathered around me, and traffic was halted while they waited for the ambulance to come and scrape me off the road. It felt like I'd had the mother of all kicks in the balls, and I lay there groaning in agony. At that time in nineteen eighty-nine, ambulance personnel weren't paramedics and only administered first aid. Anyway, I was put into the ambulance and taken back to the hospital I'd left half an hour before. As I was wheeled into A and E on a stretcher the department Sister, Alison Challenger said "Oh hello" as she recognised me. I gave a pained smile; I had been at school with Alison, so I was a little embarrassed.

At that time, I was married to Ronny (Veronica) who worked in the blood bank at the hospital. One of my colleagues in the porter's room telephoned her to break the news of my accident. She said that it was the worst ten minutes of her life coming down to casualty as she had no idea what state I was going to be in. Injuries wise, it was all soft tissue, the soft tissue being my testicles. My legs were black from where they'd caught the handlebars and my balls from where they'd impacted on the fuel tank. During my flying over the handlebars, my scrotum caught the ignition key which got bent. That gave me a nasty cut. I was very lucky that in the main my injuries were just bruises that would eventually settle down. For a few weeks it felt as if someone was swinging on my testicles while pulling my insides through my backside. Eventually once everything had healed, I was back to normal and after the bike was repaired, I was back in the saddle. A little while after that I bought a new bike – it had a bit more pizzazz than the previous one with a chrome exhaust and king and queen seat. It was in deep red and had a teardrop petrol tank. It was a lovely looking bike, but I was a more cautious rider after the accident, I rode it for a good while, but it wasn't quite the same so eventually I decided my biking days were over. I valued my crown jewels too much.

Quite a few of us rode motorcycles to work in the late eighties and on occasions would go for a ride down to the sea wall or the lighthouse on the Severn estuary. We'd take binoculars with us because at that time RAF Caerwent was still an active airbase with the United States Air Force based there. Planes, usually Harriers, C-130 (Hercules) transport planes and Chinook helicopters would fly up the coast, so we'd have a free air show. The end of the cold war put paid to that. The Americans left and the base was closed. It is still owned by the Ministry of Defence and is now used as a training and exercise area, although in twenty-twenty three there was talk of turning it into a barracks after the closure of Beachley Barracks near Chepstow.

I was there one time with Billy Saville, he'd forgotten his binoculars, so we shared mine between us. I was casually scanning the skies when I turned and looked down the sea wall. I thought I'd play a prank on Billy. "Cor Billy, there's a girl down there taking her top off, she's got a massive pair of tits". I lowered the binoculars to find that we'd been joined by a middle-aged couple who were looking at me in disbelief. I was somewhat embarrassed.

6

On the night shift once all the routine work was completed, at around one o'clock in the morning we'd settle down and try to get some kip. We'd put two chairs together and curl up to sleep, getting up to do the odd job as necessary. Phil Rogers would get a stretcher mattress off a trolley in the corridor and with a pillow, sheets and blankets he would make a kind of private bedroom under the very large table. He would make a curtain from the sheets and settle to sleep in his own private booth.

 Whenever the phone rang the light would be turned on waking everyone up. We found an old Anglepoise lamp and located a bulb for it (we nicked it from a bulkhead lamp). Our idea (Okay, it was mine) was to place the lamp close to the table the surface of which was made of light blue Formica and that would give a soft glow so that the main light didn't need to be turned on. This worked very well for a long time until the bulb went. We procured another bulb; I can't remember from where and we settled for the night as usual. During the night there was a loud crack sound, somebody muttered "What was that?". The main light went on and after a bit of a discussion and search, we couldn't find where it came from. We just put it down to the usual old building night-time sounds. We didn't check the lamp. When we woke in the morning, we went to put the lamp away to find a lampshade size hole burnt into the surface of the table. When we looked at the bulb it was a hundred and fifty watts, nearly twice the power of the original bulb. The hole was the same size as an ashtray (as I said, you could smoke anywhere back then) which we placed over the hole to disguise the damage. The porters coming in on the next shift asked us "What did you do that for?" as if we'd did it on purpose!

 As I said earlier, most of us on my shift had a motorbike and we'd park them under the canopy by the mortuary which was across the car park from the porter's room rear entrance. We had all settled down as it was a quiet night. It was in the summertime and was quite warm, so the big sash windows were open. I was sprawled over two chairs and, in my half-sleep I could hear voices coming from over where the bikes were parked. I got up and went to investigate thinking someone was trying to steal them. There was a short run of steps leading up from the porter's room to the car park. As I climbed the steps, I could hear a bit of a commotion coming from the other side.

Firemen in breathing apparatus were running around with hoses and a turntable ladder was extended to the top of the hospital C block. I rushed back to the porter's room to wake the others. "Quick lads, we'd better get up, the hospital is on fire". Nobody moved, they thought I was messing around. Eventually I persuaded them that it was true. For some reason the fire alarms hadn't sounded so we merrily carried on sleeping. Of course, with something like this happening the powers that would be all over the hospital and although everyone knew we slept, it was frowned upon.

D Block with C Block behind

It turned out that a motor in the lift housing had caught fire and was brought under control quite quickly. Of course, it meant that we never got much sleep that night, so the kettle went on and it was cards around the table. Talking of sleeping on duty, one time when I was the blood porter, I was in the land of nod when the pager started beeping. Half asleep I phoned the number which was the accident and emergency department. It was to collect samples to go to the labs. When I arrived at the department a nurse said, "We've been paging you for a while, you were sleeping weren't you?" I looked into her eyes. "No" I replied. She looked back into mine. "Liar, I can see the blanket marks on the side of your face". Touché! NHS blankets have a honeycomb pattern that had transferred onto the side of my face and my hair was a little on the bedraggled side.

I was the blood porter on the same shift as Billy, Gary, Glyn and Phil who was the chargehand and others, so we were a close-knit crew. We were based in the general porter's room situated in the centre of A block. and as I mentioned before, there were the porters in the casualty department, in addition there were a couple in the maternity wing, B block. Gary Burns was one of the "gynae" crew and would pop down to the main room during the night. When I'd moved to Velindre Hospital Garry came to my department as a patient, unfortunately I was away so never got to see him. He died not long after.

We would get up to all sorts of high jinks to pass the time on nights. While I'm talking about porters in the maternity wing, it was normally crewed by two "gynae" porters per shift who were based in a lodge at the entrance. During the daytime there were a few other porters for the small outpatient's department that led off the entrance and there was another based down in the antenatal clinic during the day. One of the gynae crew had a porter, James Johnson (name changed) who was what could only be described as odd. He gave the nurses the creeps and would always be hovering around them chatting, but you could see they were just being polite. On many occasions I "rescued" them by saying someone was wanting to see them urgently, to which they'd get away. He had worked there for many years until one day he mentioned to a student nurse that her TV was in a funny position. The hospital was a teaching hospital with its own school until the nineteen-nineties with nurse's residences at the back of the hospital. The thing was she lived on the first floor. She didn't think anything of it until she told a colleague what he'd said. Hospital security found him at a later time in the car park of the residences, off shift with a set of ladders on the roof of his car.

He was dismissed from his post; I don't know whether he was prosecuted but we never heard anything more about him.

As I've mentioned earlier, we'd explore the tunnels under the hospital, we'd also on occasions, have wheelchair races in the main corridor during quiet periods. Hospitals in those days had specific visiting hours and the corridors were nearly always deserted in between times. There was a place over in B block maternity entrance that had been dubbed the ponderosa because the visitors would be corralled in there until the doors were opened for visiting hours.

Occasionally on an afternoon or night shift we'd borrow a portable telly from A1 East and either play on the computer or if I brought my VHS (remember them?) recorder in we'd hire a film or two and watch those. Sometimes if there was a football match on or some other sport, we'd borrow the telly for that, although I didn't really have an interest in sport.

One time the next shift on told us to leave the telly and they would take it back to the A1 East for us. A couple of days later we had a phone call from the ward, could they have the telly back. We searched the entire hospital looking for this portable TV that seemed to have vanished into thin air. Days went by while we asked everyone on the other shifts if they'd seen it. It turned out that one of the porters following our shift decided to take it home with him. TVs in those days were high value goods and there was an urban myth about how the nurses were watching TV in the common room in the nurse's home and a guy in overalls came in and said the telly had to go for servicing. The telly was never seen again. May have been true but I have my suspicions. The porter brought it back once we told him it will become common knowledge if he didn't. We made some excuse to the ward, but it was difficult to get them to loan us it again.

7

In the A block main corridor of the original hospital, were plaques dedicated to some of the surgeons and staff who'd served at the hospital or in the wars. When the old building was demolished, I think these plaques were removed and put into storage in another part of the ducts that was used by the painting and decorating department. I'd like to think that these memorials are still in existence and will be displayed somewhere again, possibly in the town museum. I used to look at these plaques and try to imagine what the people to whom they refer were like. I can remember one because he had an unusual name Victor Adolphus Crinks, I think he was a surgeon in the early days of the hospital. One of the plaques was dedicated to a surgeon, it may have been Mr Crinks I'm not sure, who'd contracted blood poisoning whilst carrying out his duties as an Honorary Surgeon and had died. Honorary surgeon – I hope he was medically qualified! There was quite a few of those plaques and memorials adorning the walls of the old A block, I remember them being removed and the painters and decorators assured me that they were being stored in the basement for protection. These plaques are fascinating historical references that I hope are not lost.

The original hospital

The hospital was founded by Sir Anthony Garrod Thomas and a bust on a pedestal stood in the main entrance.

Sir Anthony Garrod Thomas

The entrance was now in use for the general public and mere mortals such as me were allowed through the front of the hospital, the offices either side inside the entrance were now used for administration. I will have more to say about the bust on the pedestal later.

The main porter's room was situated off the main thoroughfare up a short corridor and up some steps, the head porter's office was at the bottom of the steps. Opposite were toilet facilities and a small kitchen area, next to that a service lift was just off the main corridor.

As the building was almost a hundred years old there were problems from vermin and cockroaches. Some bright spark decided that if anyone saw a cockroach, they'd have to fill in a form. One morning I had just come out of the room when I spotted a large beast walking along the edge by the wall. I let it get on with its day, went and did my job and came back whereupon I mentioned the beastie. I was given the form to fill in. One of the questions asked, "Where was the cockroach going when you saw it?" Too good an opportunity to miss I wrote, "I think it was going shopping as it had a couple of bags with it". I can be so facetious at times!

One of the most feared people in the hospital were the number sevens, the nursing officers or in the good old days the Matron. We had one number seven (I don't know why they were called that; it may have been a local thing) who I thought would look good in an SS uniform – Miss Smithers (name changed). She had the face for it. I was in the gent's loo one time and on the wall, someone had written "Smithers was yer", which amused me. I'll come back to Miss Smithers in a moment.

For some reason the porter's room was moved to one of the offices in the front entrance and the head porter's office in the room opposite. I think this might have been in the latter days of the old hospital. Anyway, a large reception desk was built from low grade wood and one of the hospital's decorators, Charlie painted it and with skill, varnished it to look like it was made from quality oak or something similar. People always commented on what a lovely piece of wood it was, and we always went to great pains to tell them how it was done. It might have looked like real oak, but we always felt that Charlie needed to be recognised for his skill in making it look good.

One night shift, a gang of us were larking about in the main entrance in the middle of the night. The bust of Sir Anthony stood proudly on its pedestal at the entrance, so we decided that we'd dress him up. We placed a mop on his head to give him a wig. A fag butt was stuck in his mouth and a sack truck placed in front of him. Funny though it was it lacked a certain something, the pedestal gave the game away.

I had a bright idea to put my white coat around the shoulders and place the arms over the sack truck handles. Perfect! It looked hilarious, I had a camera with me so took some pictures, unfortunately they were a little on the dark side, but I still have them somewhere. Sir Anthony was probably spinning in his grave.

Anyway, we were all laughing and joking when someone said "Quick, Miss Smithers is coming" to which everybody scattered and left me to face the music. I didn't have time to run because my white coat was around the shoulders of the bust. She glared at the head on the pedestal while saying something about it being disrespectful. I just stood there and said I'd only just got there myself and would sort it out. I'm not entirely sure she believed me, had she looked at the white coat it had my name badge on it and my pager was in the pocket, luckily it hadn't gone off. I can't remember what she had come down the corridor for but as luck would have it, I'd got away with it. I really thought at that point my career in the NHS was going to be over.

There were other porters covering the hospital on days as well as the rotating or continental shifts. One "day" porter who had worked at the hospital for many years was Charlie, a popular character. He wore a long grey porter's coat with the sleeves rolled up and big boots plodding everywhere like a pantomime villain. One daytime the phone rang, and Charlie got up to answer the call. "Porters" he proclaimed in his breathy tone. He nodded and answered "Yes" several times and finished the call with "OK, I'm on my way" then placed the phone back on the hook. He headed for the door with his usual plod then stopped and turned back heading towards the phone. Most of the boys were sat around the table playing cards or drinking tea, watched as Charlie stopped and thought to himself. He plodded back to the phone and just as he was about to pick it up it rang. "Porters" he proclaimed again. The person on the other end said something and Charlie replied in his old man voice "I was just going to ring you to find out who you were". We were all in stitches with laughter. Poor Charlie worked as a porter for very many years but never got to retire as he became ill with a brain tumour and passed away.

A regular patient at the hospital was the celebrated actor Anthony Hopkins's mother, Muriel. She had diabetes so was admitted when her diabetes was out of control. One time she was brought into A1 East and Anthony visited her on numerous occasions. One of the boys got talking to him and invited him to the porter's room for a coffee. When he'd finished visiting his mum he called in for the coffee and stayed for about half an hour chatting. Before he left, he signed the corner of the notice board with "All good wishes to all in the porter's room, Anthony Hopkins".

When the hospital was being demolished, I did toy with the idea of cutting that section off to keep for posterity, in hindsight, I wish I had but there you go, it went the way of the rubble. Anthony Hopkins was at the time a Patron of the of the Diabetes Centre, which was situated in Richmond House, a mansion in the grounds of the hospital.

8

One sunny day I had just arrived at work and seemed to be having a quiet shift with very few calls, so I thought I'd take a walk down to casualty and sit around outside and enjoy the sunshine. I noted as I went past the waiting area how unusually quiet it was. As I went out through the ambulance bay, I could see Doug Sharp ducked down behind a parked car looking towards the main gate. "Hiya Doug, what's going on?" I called out while boldly striding across the car park. "There's a man with a gun in that car down there" he replied. I looked down towards the gates of the hospital to see police cars all parked with officers ducked behind the vehicles. A couple officers were waving at me to keep back. There was a man in the back seat of the car with a gun trained on the driver and me standing in the open. I immediately dived down next to Doug.

The Newport siege went on for three days and moved around the Newport area culminating in shots being fired by what was the Kings Head Hotel at the top end of town in Newport. It was all over the National news, and I encountered it several times over the three days as it moved to places around the town on my journey home, invariably I'd get home and watch it on the news. The man fired the gun just scraping the driver and the siege was over. He had a sawn-off shotgun with a rope hoop tied to it, the hoop was around the driver's neck. The driver was very lucky and got away with just minor injuries. It turned out that it was all over a woman. The hostage was having a fling with the man's wife. These things never end well but at least there were no fatalities.

Working in a district general hospital you get to see quite a slice of life from the good to the bad to the very bad. At the start of my night shift I went down to the casualty ambulance bay one sunny evening and was just milling about waiting for a call and I could sense a certain sombre atmosphere, I'd only just come on shift so was waiting for my first call. The Perspex flap doors to the resuscitation unit opened and a nurse came out carrying a small child of about eight over her shoulder covered in a blanket, a mop of hair was just showing over the top. She was taking him to the mortuary and didn't want him to be taken in the mortuary trolley through the hospital. This way was shorter and quicker. I don't know the circumstances of his passing; I really couldn't imagine what the parents were going through but it's an image that has stayed with me my entire time in the health service and beyond.

As I wore a white coat (a short jacket known as an intern's jacket) I was often called doctor, especially as I carried a pager. This happened quite a lot throughout my time in the NHS as I still got called doctor right up until I retired.

A patient once called me doctor and I corrected him to which he replied, "Well you have the air of a doctor". That was just my level of professionalism!

I'd be walking down the corridor and a visitor would say to me "Excuse me, Doctor" if they were asking for directions or something else. Most of the time it was easier just to answer their query without correcting them but being mistaken for or called a doctor was a frequent occurrence. It must be noted that sometimes lay people, that is people who don't know how hospitals work think that men are doctors and women are nurses regardless of their job or so it seemed. Certainly was the case with patients from a certain era. Once I was working in endoscopy and I'd suffered a muscle spasm in my neck resulting in me having limited movement. One of the registrars sorted a prescription for me so off I went down to the pharmacy department. I handed in the script and took a seat with a few members of the public who were also waiting. A few minutes later, a pharmacy assistant stuck her head out of the hatch and called "Doctor Stacey" to which all eyes were on me, I just stood up with a "yes" and took the bag with my prescription and left. It was just easier than standing there explaining that I wasn't a doctor.

Currently in Wales at the time of writing they have The All-Wales Uniform policy which is supposed to colour code all NHS workers. Everybody wears scrubs which are the colour of your designation, for instance in my job as a Clinical Technologist I would be wearing black as that is the colour for medical imaging so radiographers would wear the same colour. Nurses wear blue in different shades, light blue for staff nurses, royal blue for specialist nurses. Student nurses wear purple, senior nurses wear navy while domestic staff wear red.

The upshot to this uniform policy is that the general public see you in scrubs they think you are a doctor. I personally loved the good old days when you had a uniform to be proud of. Some of the scrubs you see in hospitals these days look like they just took them from the laundry and didn't bother to iron them. They just look so scruffy. In terms of uniform, I really think standards have slipped. When I was a porter in the Royal Gwent there was a painter and decorator called John who, every time he saw me kept calling me Prof. "Hi Prof. How's it going?" I tried to correct him, but he never changed. Hospitals had their own painting and decorating departments way back then but now this task is performed by outside contractors. Everything these days must go out to tender as they call it, not necessarily a good thing. Personally, I think pockets get lined and the rich get richer.

9

In the late nineteen-eighties, a rapist was at large in the Newport area that had everyone on the lookout for anyone that might be the suspect. One daytime I was on my way to a call and made my way to the third floor of the hospital, this led to all the other blocks. I was going to collect blood samples from the wards in B block. The lift door opened and as I exited a man ran towards me catch the lift, so I held the door for him to get in. The door closed and as I set off a group of men in suits followed by two police in uniform who also ran towards me. "Did you see a man in a black jacket come this way?" The man that I'd held the door open for, had a few minutes previously held a knife to the throat of one of the catering staff. They continued their chase by taking another lift. I found out later that he wasn't the rapist just a nutter going berserk in the canteen kitchens. The knife it turned out was an ordinary cutlery knife that wasn't very sharp. He was beaten off by other staff members and legged it to the lifts whereupon I aided his escape, unintentionally of course. He was eventually caught and sectioned, the rapist was at large for a few more days before he too was apprehended.

When I first took on the blood porters' job, there were no such things as vacutainers and urine samples were taken in pots with a metal lid that wasn't exactly leak proof. Blood samples were taken in a syringe and squirted into the sample tube that had a screw on lid. Not the best but that's the way it was. Samples weren't put into plastic bags for transport as they are these days.
 In the late nineteen-eighties a virus was doing the rounds and seemed to be affecting mainly gay men. HIV had everybody worried and none more so than healthcare workers who would be handling the blood or looking after infected patients. Nobody knew at the time that it couldn't be passed on unless it was in direct contact with body fluids. Anyway, all samples started to be placed in plastic bags for transport to the laboratory. Not taking any chances, and in innocence, if a patient was suspected of being HIV positive, samples would be double bagged with a yellow label. Prior to the rise of the virus there was many a time I carried samples loose to the laboratory with the awful feeling of some yucky substance running down my arm. I would be scrubbing my arms thoroughly with the strongest cleaning product I could find including Vim, a domestic bleach cleaning powder.

Samples for biochemistry would be accompanied by a white request card of about ten by eight inches in size. I was called one afternoon to collect some samples from the casualty department and had a few of these cards in my hand. The pathology department was accessed on the fourth floor of C block and to get to it there was a corrugated fibreglass tunnel that had translucent windows. The tunnel went from A block (the old Victorian part) into the basement of C block. From here I would take the lift to the fourth floor and on to another link corridor to the pathology department. There were four lifts for passengers and three on the opposite side for goods or patient transport. The button to call the lift was towards the other end of the basement. You could see if a lift was there by looking for its light in the gap of the doors and, by sliding a card into the gap the "magic eye" would open the doors thus saving you the walk to the button. I'd used this technique many times but this one time as I slid the pathology request cards into the gap and the lift suddenly took off with cards in tow. So, there I was left holding a pile of samples as the cards disappeared into the lift shaft. I never did come clean as to what happened, I just took the samples to the lab reception and left them on the reception desk. I was questioned about it but told them that I'd left them on the main pathology desk. I heard nothing more about it. The lab would have phoned, and new cards would have been sent. I often wonder if those cards are still in the lift shaft with thirty odd years of dust on them.

 Early one morning just as I'd come on shift, I had a call from resus which at that time had moved into a new extension that had been built in the C block car park. The message was to collect a blood sample and take it to the lab. I entered the unit and it was very quiet as there was nobody around except a patient lying on a trolley asleep. I thought it unusual for a patient to be left alone like that especially in resus. I looked at the patient and thought he didn't look too well so I looked at the blood form. In the clinical details box was written "Found dead at home", that explained why he didn't look too clever.

10

One time I was on my way to labour ward to collect some blood samples when I got as far as the main entrance to maternity when the automatic doors opened and in ran a woman with her trousers and pants round her knees. "Quick I'm having a baby" she shouted. I had a load of samples in my hand so couldn't immediately go to her aid. I told her to wait where she was while I put the samples in the porter's lodge while I went to find a chair. I took her to one of the wards and explained to the sister what had happened. I left the ward and set off back to the pathology lab. As I got to the entrance the automatic doors opened again and a man ran in. "A woman came in couple of minutes ago, she's having a baby?" I took him to the ward. All this time three pregnant ladies were sat on some seats watching the drama unfold. I eventually got the samples to the laboratory and when my workload calmed down, I went to the ward to find out the outcome. The woman was a psychiatric patient and wasn't even pregnant, the man who'd brought her in wasn't even related to her. He had been driving along minding his own business when she ran into the road and told him she needed to get to the hospital urgently. He brought her in thinking she was having a baby. The ward gave him a cup of tea, an explanation and sent him on his way. He had a great tale to tell at the pub that evening, he certainly needed a drink after that experience.

The Royal Gwent Hospital consisted of (in the early eighties) A block (the original Victorian part) which had next to it a sixties or seventies addition that contained the paediatric wards with the fracture and orthopaedic department on the ground floor. B block housed the maternity and gynaecology services that was opened in the mid-sixties. In front of that there was the satellite ante natal clinic. C block, the newer addition was situated behind A block and contained wards, theatres, pharmacy and other departments. Behind C block was the pathology department accessed via a long link corridor. Behind that was the nurse's accommodation in Friar's Fields and further up the hill was "The Friars", an old mansion that housed the post graduate department along with a few management offices. Eventually, A block was demolished to be replaced by D block. The idea was that when seen from the air the main buildings of the hospital spelt an H.

As I've said previously, floor three in C block was where other blocks and departments were accessed from, the central hub so to speak. When I first started at the hospital where the day surgery and endoscopy department is now housed contained what was called central changing. You would go to a little hatch and ask for whatever uniform you wore for work. Anybody could rock up ask for a white coat of their size and be on their way, it was unheard of that someone might pretend to be a doctor or other member of staff. This was eventually superseded by a vending machine system and sewing rooms and departments were made redundant. Floor two led to the other blocks but was more for service traffic although the X-ray department, Pharmacy and the switchboard was accessed via this floor. When the battery ran out on your pager, you'd go to the switchboard to have it replaced. You'd go in and the ladies would be sat at the old PABX switchboard knitting or watching TV answering calls as and when.

There were networks of other corridors leading off this way and that to different places, but these could change as new developments took place. There used to be a corridor opposite the Day Surgery/ Endoscopy suite that was supported on a high bridge that led to floor three of A block. This was removed when it was discovered to contain asbestos, A block was at around this time about to be condemned as the new D block was in the offing. To walk past there now you'd never know it existed. I am writing this in twenty twenty-three and haven't worked at that hospital for many years and I know a lot has changed there. A new hospital, The Grange opened in twenty-twenty and took some of the major roles of the Royal Gwent.

Anyway, I digress, I shall continue my journey through the NHS. For now, I am still in the porter's department.

11

The translucent corridor going from A to C block was to cause Billy much embarrassment and scare a member of the public. As I mentioned before I wore a white jacket in the early days as blood porter. We were loitering in the main corridor while it was quiet one evening when I got a call for one thing or another. I proceeded down the corrugated corridor and went off to do the job. In the meantime, Billy continued loitering with Gary May. As they stood in the main corridor, they could see the translucent windows of the corrugated corridor to which a person in white was walking towards them. Billy thought he'd jump out on what he thought was me only to land in front of a terrified woman in a white cardigan. Billy rather red faced had to apologise profusely. We laughed at that, but it could have had dire consequences.

As blood porter you could have a very quiet shift, or you could be rushed off your feet. Being rushed off your feet was the norm during the day, but it made the time go quicker. I used to buy cans of cola from the canteen and put them in the fridge in the porter's room. One such time I'd bought a can, but it wasn't very cold, so I placed it in the freezer box with a view to drinking it after a job. Unfortunately, in the meantime I became very busy and forgot the can in the freezer. Eventually as things quietened down, I went for the can. I gave it a gentle shake to check how frozen it was and how much fluid was inside. The ring pulls on the cans in those days were slightly different to the ones today. I pulled the ring whereupon the entire contents came out in a fountain straight into my face. Everyone was diving under tables and chairs to escape the sticky liquid that was emptying from the can. Once it was over, I was laughing so much my stomach hurt. I still say it was the best twenty-eight pence I have ever spent. I know, twenty-eight pence!

In the final days of the old hospital, I was walking along one of the corridors on my way to a job when I noticed a large crack in a wall that I knew hadn't been there before. I found one of the

maintenance people and asked him to come and take look. He took one look at it and said, "Oh dear, that doesn't look good". The A block was closed not long afterwards. I often wish that I'd taken more photos when I was there, I did take my video camera in one time on a night shift, but the footage has been lost some time ago. I'm sure someone must have taken photos inside the old hospital over the years. Medical Illustration took lots of photos for various reasons so they must have an archive somewhere.
In the porter's room all human life was there.

It was noted that some people would think that because they were porters and therefore unskilled, that they weren't particularly intelligent. That wasn't necessarily true. Some guys had worked in other careers and had maybe been made redundant and took on porters work to make ends meet. Others were using it to fund further education. Quite a few went on to other careers. One porter Danny Connikie (I think that's how it's spelled) worked for a couple of years then left to join the Metropolitan police. His mother worked in the sewing department (yes, they had one of those too in the good old days).

12

I enjoyed working in the porter's department and had some good laughs among other things but eventually it wasn't enough for me, I needed something with a bit more bite and a bit more money and possibly with a career path. I started looking on the hospital job boards to see if there was something else I could do in the hospital. A job was advertised for an Endoscopy Assistant, and I thought this had just what I was looking for. This was a new post so there was scope (pardon the pun) for developing the role. I went to the Endoscopy department for a look around and showed a lot of interest eventually getting an interview although I really can't remember having one. The job was mine, so I turned up one Monday morning in nineteen ninety-five bright eyed and bushy tailed ready for work. This was a bit more like it. With lots to learn and do, I thrived in this department which was a lot different to being a porter. The first thing as with all new jobs is to tour the department meeting members of staff and familiarisation of the layout. I was introduced to the lead consultant Dr Miles Allison who I would work under for my entire time in endoscopy. Miles was highly regarded physician who was always willing to explain the procedures and what they were looking for to nurses and the assistants such as myself which made working there even more interesting. The post was part technician and part nursing auxiliary, so it had a good variety of challenges and entailed working in the procedure room assisting with procedures and cleaning the endoscopes.

When I started the endoscopes were optical so that only the person doing the procedure could see what was happening, there were attachments to allow another person to view proceedings or to connect to a monitor although these were not ideal. After a few years a new system was introduced, EVIS, Endoscopic Video Imaging System, I took a particular interest in this so was well versed in its operation. As everything was now shown on a large screen it allowed everyone in the room to see what was happening which made the job much more interesting, and it was easier for the endoscopist to explain what he or she was doing.

Being technically minded I quickly showed my worth when problems occurred with the endoscope system and I was able to troubleshoot the problem and get the system working again, sometimes during the procedures. Usually, it was something simple like the endoscope wasn't fully plugged in or a cable had worked loose. Whenever there was a problem, the consultant would call "Get Fred." One radiologist Dr Gerald Thomas always asked how I knew what to do and how I knew what the problem was. I just had and aptitude for it and as I said, I am technically minded. The Endoscopy Department at this time was headed by Sister Sue Barker who had nursed my father on A2 East before he was moved to another hospital. The Endoscopy Suite previously had been located at the very top of A block along with Day Surgery next to A3 East.

When A block was closed Endoscopy and Day Surgery moved into a newly created suite where Central Changing used to be on the third floor. The new endoscopy unit was named after Dr Brian Calcraft who founded endoscopy services at the Royal Gwent Hospital. Sadly, and ironically, he died from bowel cancer just before I joined the endoscopy team. I knew of him as I'd seen him around the hospital, but he was gone before I started in the unit. Doctors in those days wore shirt and tie with a clean white coat and that is how I remember him. Standards have certainly fallen in certain areas nowadays. Endoscopy with other departments and was wards collectively known as the Gastroenterology Department.

Dr Brian Calcraft

So, the day had come where I was to start learning what the job entailed. As with all new jobs familiarisation and orientation were the starting point. The Calcraft Suite consisted of two endoscopy rooms/theatres, a large one and a slightly smaller one. Each had its own cleaning room and "CSSD" cupboard where things like dressings and biopsy taking equipment was stored. There was a patient beverage point next to an doctor's office which was directly outside the larger room, just inside the main door from the waiting room was the department's office where the department secretary worked.

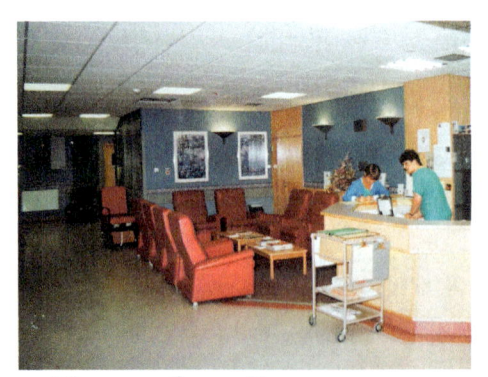

The comfy recliners

There was the patient waiting/ recovery area that had comfy reclining seats and trolley bays for sedated patients recovering from procedures. Here was the nurse's station and toilets behind that.

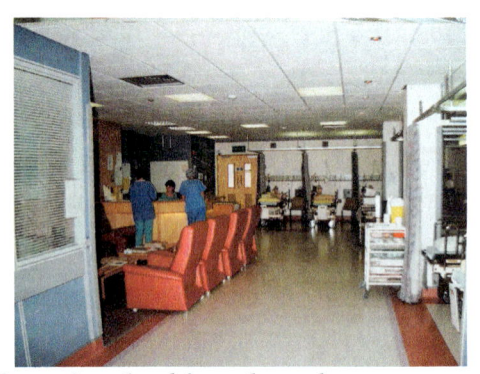

Another view looking the other way

Another small room was a patient interview room where patients were booked in and this was also the place where bad news had been broken many times including to my mother, but more on that later. Coming from the porter's department was a complete change for me as I would now be working closely alongside doctors and nurses learning quite a lot about the procedures. The consultants were only too happy to explain what was going on and how to recognise certain diseases and anatomy specifics. I had a mentor who I think was Lisa Gilby who was an experienced nurse teaching me the aspects of the job. Initially, the job was to clean the instruments and generally assist in the procedure room or recovery area but as time went on more was added to the job description. When assisting in the recovery area you would sit the patient up as they came around and make them a cup of tea with a biscuit. I enjoyed the patient contact in this way, but I wanted to do more.

Eventually I was taught to do diabetic blood checks, blood pressures and removal of butterflies and cannulas.

I enjoyed walking in my spare time and on occasions would put a poster up in the department saying where I was going and if anyone wanted to join me, they could. The department had a great team of about fifteen nurses and assistants and we used to have some great social events. Sometimes we'd go for a curry after work or maybe a drink amongst other things.

Members of the Gastroenterology Team. Standing, left to right: Angela Merrett, Sarah Knight-Beardmore, Terry Perkins, 'Manny' Srivastava, Jill Carter, Elizabeth Williams, Keith Vellacott, Miles Allison, Sue Barker, Frederick Stacey. Kneeling: Karina Mitchell, Chrissie Smith, Pamela Clarke, Gini Joseph and Denise Jenkins. Note photograph of Dr. Calcraft in the background.
(photograph Brian Peeling)

Professor Brian Peeling's photo from his book The Royal Gwent and St Woolos Hospital- A Century of Service

For the most part two consultants, Dr Allison and Dr Manny

Srivastava did procedures during the week. On certain days or half days other consultants would have a list. Tuesday mornings was the bronchoscopy list, and I think if I recall rightly, Thursday afternoon was Dr Allison's laser therapy list.

I was a Roman re-enactor in my spare time and one of the surgeons, Brian Stephenson who had a morning list one day a week in the department got wind of this. He was hosting a surgeon's dinner at the Priory Hotel at Caerleon, South Wales. As Caerleon had major Roman connections he thought it would be great if I would come along in the Roman kit to add a touch of the exotic. I did the gig but felt a bit of a Charlie, I milled about chatting to the guests and some even seemed genuinely interested. I had the dinner in full kit which was slightly uncomfortable. There was a magician performing after the dinner that left everyone wondering how he did it. I was left wondering why I did it. He asked if I would do it again but unfortunately, I was unavailable.

I lived alone after my divorce from Ronny, and I ran a mobile disco that brought in a little bit of income, petty cash. The nurses and doctors were always having events of some description and I was booked for most of these gigs that usually took place at Pill Harriers Social club not far from the hospital.

Living on my own I did find that at times I was lonely. It was great if there were things going on such as nights out but when I'd go to work and come home to an empty house, it started to get me down.

One Christmas time I was for whatever reason, going to be spending it on my own.

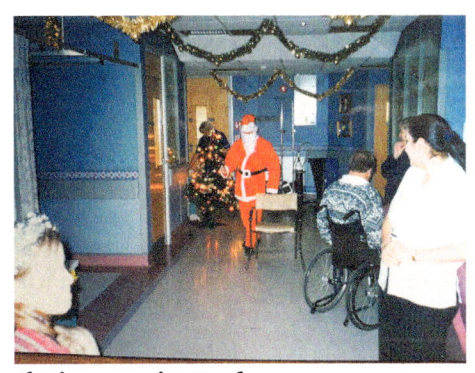

Christmas in Endoscopy

I wasn't too worried about it and set about getting my Christmas dinner sorted. As I said I worked with a fabulous group of girls and Chrissie Smith invited me to spend Boxing Day with her husband Nigel and her two daughters, Emily and Sophie which I thoroughly enjoyed. I had a lovely friendship with Chrissie and Nigel but sadly she passed away from breast cancer. When I'd moved to Velindre Hospital she came to our department for scans. Two weeks before she passed, she was at Velindre to see her consultant and she sent a text to see if I was about. I saw her quite tearful in the outpatients waiting room not realising that would be the last time I'd see her.

Chrissie on the right

Chrissie was the life and soul of the party and would be the first up on the dance floor. She joined Channel Four's Stand Up to Cancer with the Big C Choir and sang with them at the Albert Hall. I interviewed her about it on my radio show. Chrissie is much missed by everyone who knew her.

Anyway, back to endoscopy, while I was there, I joined the Nursing bank as a Nursing Auxiliary to help pay my bills. Endoscopy Assistant pay wasn't great, better than porter's pay but not by much. It helped but I discovered nursing wasn't for me. I had people sick on me, old ladies peeing on my shoes and in the good old days the hospital had a barber, but once they'd done away with them shaving people's bits, it was down to the NA.

I once had a run in with an NA who worked permanently on this one ward. She just saw me as someone who'd come to steal her job. As I told her, she could keep her job as I wasn't going to be doing it any longer. I stopped working on the bank soon after but before that on a night shift on a different ward after all the observations had been done and the patients had settled down, I sat down at the nurse's station. I was chatting to this one nurse when another nurse walked past the desk with a mattress and pillow from a trolley. "Where is she going?" I asked in case she needed me to help. "She's going into the bathroom to get some sleep" she replied. "Why don't you go with her and have a snooze". I respectfully declined, I had never met her before, I couldn't go sleeping next to her. I went and paid a visit to the porter's room.

Back on the endoscopy unit during the day someone said to me, "Why don't you do your nurse training?". No thanks, it just wasn't for me. I could do the simple stuff on endoscopy like blood pressures and removing butterflies but anything else was just too much. Having said that, we would sometimes have emergency endoscopies on the department. Then it was all hands to the pump so to speak.

When cleaning the trolleys afterwards you sometimes find yourself arm deep in some grim bodily fluids or other. The worst was if a patient had a bleed from the rear end called a melaena, this was caused by ingested blood if a patient had an internal bleed. It had a particular aroma that could make you heave.

Enough of the gory stuff, but still talking about emergencies. I had to go to one of the wards to check a patient had been prepped for a procedure the next day. When I left the department, the place was busy with patients waiting for their procedures and others on trolleys recovering. I left the department for literally twenty minutes. When I returned the place was like the Marie Celeste, all the patients had gone.

I went to find someone to find out what was going on. Sister Sue Barker came through the main doors. What's happening?" I asked, "Where is everyone?". "Go and have a look in theatre" she replied. I opened the door to the endoscopy room and the only light was from the escape lights. All the equipment had been removed and water was pouring in through the suspended ceiling. A pipe had burst so all the lists for that day had been cancelled.

There was surgeon called Ken Shute who had a regular list one morning a week. He could be a bit of a tartar but was always ok with me, he was one of those consultants that wanted his patients in bed ready for when he did his ward round.

Sometimes I'd see him in the street driving his car and he'd always give a wave. I recall one time I was working in the recovery area of the department and Mr Shute had his list in the main room. He had a student in with him to watch the procedures. A nurse came out of theatre for something or other because the student had fainted. I opened the procedure room door to see Mr Shute lifting and lowering the student's legs to pump blood into her brain. It was an amusing sight.

We had quite a few students in the department to observe the procedures and fainting was a regular occurrence. I remember one time assisting with a procedure alongside one of the doctors and Heather McGregor was the nurse looking after the patient. A student was present and was the sister of one of the doctors in the hospital. The procedure was going quite swimmingly when suddenly there was an almighty bang. The student had fainted flat on her back and cracked her head on the floor. Heather and I looked at each other with an Ooooh!, so sympathetic.

We couldn't leave the patient having the procedure, so we called for another nurse who went to her aid. The student was kept in the department on a trolley for observations for most of the day. I bet she had the mother of all headaches from that.

One time a small group of medical students was watching Dr Allison performing a procedure and once it was over, he was explaining a few points to them. The female student stood there looking indifferent and chewing on gum which I thought was so disrespectful. I could imagine if that had happened in days of old her feet wouldn't have touched the ground. You can call me old fashioned if you like but I really do think standards are falling.

The cleaning room was through a door off the procedure room and contained two cleaning machines and a cleaning bath. The endoscopes were first given a basic clean before being brought into this room. Then after a thorough clean would be put into the washing machines for sterilisation. The room had a powerful extractor because of the toxic chemicals used for cleaning.

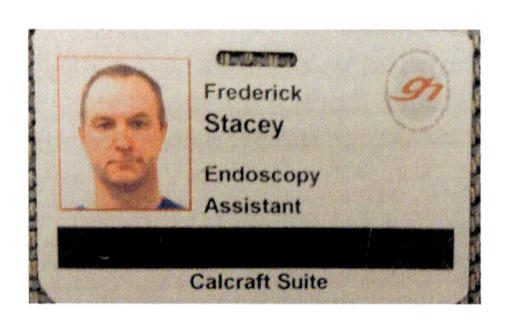

13

I was on holiday in Saundersfoot on the coast with Ronny, my daughter and my mother, we were staying in an apartment for a week. A couple of days in we were having a meal when my mother started choking. We'd sorted her out and made sure she was ok. It turned out she'd had been having these episodes for a little while. We asked my sister Carol to sort an appointment with her GP, as my mother went to her house for lunch every day. This she did and she was given an appointment to see a specialist, who referred her to Miles Allison, the lead consultant in our department. On the day she came in I was working in recovery while she went in to have the endoscopy. She was brought into recovery, where I kept an eye on her.

Once she was awake and had a cup of tea, she dressed and was sat in the comfy chairs. I knew something wasn't right when they asked us to go into the patient interview room and Dr Allison would be in to see us. It was cancer, quite advanced and although they would give her treatment ultimately it was terminal. I was very upset, so Sister Barker told me along with my sister Helen to take her home. My mam visited our department regularly for months having laser treatment and she was eventually fitted with an oesophageal stent – a wire mesh that opened the oesophagus to allow food to pass to the stomach. This was one of the last things to happen and had limited success. My mam was admitted to B3 East, which was over the maternity end of the hospital, this ward was originally part of maternity services, but the hospital was starting to repurpose some of the wards and departments. My mam was there for a few weeks before passing away.

The girls in the department were immensely supportive to me during this period as not only had I lost my Mam, but I was going through my divorce and buying a house, the three most stressful things in life apparently, they saw me through and for that I am eternally grateful to them. I was given as much time as I needed but me being me just got on with it. Sister Barker did ask if I'd had enough time off, but I had.

14

I had gone to the ward again to see a patient before their procedure. When I left the waiting area was full with patients recovering from their procedures or waiting to go in, I wasn't gone long. I came back to the department to find it empty of patients and staff yet again. I went into the procedure room to find that empty too. Next port of call was through into Day Surgery to see if they knew where everyone was. That was empty too except for one of the Operating Department Assistants who told me that everyone had gone to main theatre as there had been a major incident. I arrived at the recovery room of the theatre suite where everyone was being briefed. "Ah Fred, you're used to sorting blood for theatres, you can be blood products coordinator". With that they slapped an apron on me with "Blood Products" written across it.
The incident was a coach carrying disabled passengers that had careered off the road through the middle of a roundabout and had landed on its side. We waited expecting it to become extremely busy. As we waited for news from the accident and emergency department, we chatted amongst ourselves, someone higher up was being informed of proceedings, but the ordinary foot soldiers as always were kept in the dark. After an hour or so we were told we could stand down, there were a few casualties but not the large number or bad injuries that was initially expected, so we all went back to the endoscopy department.

Sister Sue Barker, Nurse Sue Palin and I decided that we would like to have an allotment, so we found one available in Cwmbran, a town near Newport. The idea was that we'd grow vegetables and possibly some fruit. Any excess would be shared with the department, the image crossed my mind of cabbages and runner beans wrapped in newspaper being palmed off on everyone in the department whether they wanted them or not.

At the allotment the ground was rough as the plot hadn't been used for some time, we started in earnest to clear the ground and turn the soil over and remove the multitude of weeds that was growing there. We realised that it was going to be a mammoth task so we decided we'd hire a rotavator that would break up the soil. It had some success, but it was difficult to get it to completely do what we wanted. After several months of toil and the realisation that the plot wasn't the best in the allotment, due to time constraints and other reasons we eventually let the plot go.

I heard years later from Lisa that Sue Palin had passed away; I don't know the reason but was quite upset and shocked about it as Sue was a lovely person and not very old, probably in her fifties. I got on well with Sue as did everyone in the department.

Lisa a Staff nurse started in the department about a year or so after me. I was going through my divorce at this time and was buying a house that just happened to be in the next street to Lisa. We gravitated to each other and eventually ended up going out together. Sadly, it was not to be, and we went our separate ways. We're still friends and in touch through Facebook and I have met up with her a couple times since usually for someone's retirement. Endoscopy had a good social life with all or some of us going out regularly perhaps to the cinema, a meal or just for drinks after work. Christmas was always on the agenda with the department Christmas "do" being planned from around November time or sometimes earlier. We had some great parties or meals for the festive season, but one of the best was when the consultants decided they would take us out to The Celtic Manor for a meal. It had been a fantastic evening the like of which few of us could afford to repeat.

It was in endoscopy that I ended up going on a hen party. Sarah Knight was getting married, so all the girls were going to Torquay for an overnight stay. I was invited much to some's annoyance and in hindsight wish I hadn't gone with them. I was living with an Irish girl Geraldine at this time. I drove to Torquay taking a couple of hens with me including Geraldine. Next morning, after an evening on the sauce I was a little worse for wear. I arrived at breakfast in the hotel looking and feeling like death warmed up, I had my food and went back to bed to sleep it off. By midday I was back to normal and ready to enjoy the day, well, half a day around Torquay. I can't remember the return journey, but I must have driven the hens back home. I have photographs of the evening so I must have taken a camera with me, of course this was before phones had decent cameras, so I took a compact film camera. Imagine that real film, the only thing with phone photos is they rarely get printed and after a year or so with changes of phone end up getting lost.

15

During my time in endoscopy, as mentioned earlier I also ran a mobile disco providing my services to most of the hospital's parties which usually took place at Pill Harriers Social Club not far from the hospital. The money from this helped to grease the wheels of life.

I'd get home from a day in work, load up the car with all the gear, get to the venue unload everything (you could rely on the actual venue being upstairs and at the other end of the room) then you'd set up, do the show, load all the gear into the car again then get home unload the car and get up the next morning for work and people would say all you do is play a few records. I did get annoyed when people would ask if I'd do it for free. There was one time when I did a doctor's bash in St Woolos Hospital which is just up the hill from the Royal Gwent. They had a break in the middle for karaoke. I didn't offer karaoke, so they got someone to come in do it for an hour or so then I'd carry on with the disco. I charged eighty quid, and the karaoke guy charged a hundred. When it came time for him to go, they shelled out his money no problem at all, when it came to me, they ummed and arred. They kept on persuading me to carry on even though I had to be up for work the next day, but I bled them dry of money to the point that they would have to go to the cash point across the road. I finished around three in the morning. I wasn't keen to do doctor's parties after that although the lure of cash did see me doing a few more including a Registrar's ball at The Celtic Manor.

The money from these gigs was useful petty cash, but it was sporadic and couldn't be relied upon. To help make ends meet and to see if I could make a career as a nurse, I mentioned earlier that I joined the nursing bank as a nursing auxiliary. If I had spare time, I'd do a shift at the Royal Gwent Hospital or at St Woolos which was mainly care of the elderly and as I mentioned was just up the hill from the Gwent. Some shifts were okay but in the main it wasn't for me. Old ladies peeing on my shoes and taking on the role of surgical barber shaving blokes pubes before their ops did not endear me to that career path. So, I continued with the day job and the odd disco supplementing my income.

I was managing well on my own paying my mortgage and bills while sustaining myself. Then suddenly, I don't know how, I found one month that I couldn't pay my mortgage. I was with Lloyds Bank at this time and my mortgage was with the Halifax. I thought I'd better let the bank know. Lloyds bank in Newport were about as much help as a chocolate teapot. So, I thought it best to have a word with the Halifax. Boom, they were extremely helpful and sorted out the problem there and then. I moved all my finances to the Halifax right at that moment and have been quite happy since. I am detracting off the path slightly, when I was having this slight financial hiccup, Sister Barker offered to help me which was very kind of her and shows you the close team that we were. I declined as I could never borrow from a friend.

16

I did enjoy living on my own, the freedom to do whatever I wanted was great but there were times when I felt seriously lonely. I just needed someone to be there and to talk to. I turned to what was at the time the early stages of internet dating. Of course, at this time the internet used what was known as dial up, there was no such thing as broadband, everything came down a phone landline. If you wanted to see a picture it would load line by line and take an age.

I found it was much easier for a woman to get a date on internet dating than a bloke called Fred. The name conjures up images of an old bloke in flat cap and slippers and anyone who knows me will know that is far from the real me. With that I didn't want to lie by calling myself a completely different name, but I had to call myself something else, so I used the latter part of my name and called myself Rick. I was out with a girl one day and I was looking at something and she was trying to attract my attention. Of course, I wasn't used to being called Rick, so I was completely oblivious. That relationship didn't last long, probably about three months which was about the norm for dates. If it went beyond three months, then it was possibly going to be a goer. I was signed up to a site that predated Facebook by a few years that was more like a chat room combined with a dating site.

It was okay but it seemed to be full of social misfits, and no, I wasn't one of them! It served a turn until Facebook came along and I met an Irish girl, Geraldine who lived on Jersey in the Channel Islands. She invited me over and I was travelling back and forth to Jersey every other weekend. Geraldine was a writer and business guru so had a lot of free time.

To make friends and to get me out of the house, I became an army cadet instructor, and the officers gave me the nickname Bergerac after the TV detective series based on Jersey. Geraldine eventually moved in with me and we cohabited for two years. Imagine that, from Jersey to Newport. Shame it wasn't the other way round.

Sadly, it was not to be, I just wasn't feeling it. Geraldine left and there I was alone again.

One of the things about working in an environment that was predominantly female was the fact they talked about everything regardless if I was present or not. They did say that they'd forget I was there. I was working on the nurse's station with another nurse when she went around the corner to the lockers. There was a bit of fumbling, a couple of pffts then she locked the locker and came and sat back down. She sat there for a few moments then turned towards me and said, "Can you smell my Charlie from over there?". We both burst out laughing once she realised what she'd said.

The job in endoscopy was going well with various courses being completed, the main one was KeyMed Part One and was a two-day course for nurses and technicians at the endoscope manufacturers base in Southend. I learnt a lot from that course, and it proved useful during the job as it gave me a greater understanding of the instrument's anatomy.

Endoscopy was an interesting job and I enjoyed working there enormously and some of the friends I made there are still in touch through Facebook.

The junior doctors used to do a clinic every Tuesday morning called the H Pylori Breath Test Clinic where patients undergo a test to find out if they are affected by the Helicobacter Pylori bacteria that can cause stomach problems. It was determined that it was too simple a task for doctors to perform and their skills could be used elsewhere, so the powers that be thought nurses could do the task freeing up the doctors for other work. The nurses decided they didn't want to do it either so after a lot of debate as to whether an assistant was legally able to carry out the test it was decided that I could do it. I got into my stride with it ordering kits and performing the tests and sending off the bags of air to Llandough Hospital for testing.

As part of the pre-test checks I'd have to ask the patient if they'd followed the instructions to stop taking certain meds plus other checks. One young lady came in and I opened her notes. I was looking at her whilst going through the checklist when she drew my attention to the notes, I looked down to see that the file had fallen open on two photographs. The photos were head and shoulders shots of her with her breasts on display. I closed the notes offering my apologies, she explained why the photos were taken but I can't remember why. She wasn't fazed by it. I could feel my face redden and just got on with the test.

A few doctors and consultants turned up to have the test and one surgeon, the old school type with a pin stripe suit and coloured hanky in the breast pocket kept asking questions even though he as a senior surgeon should have known the answers. Why do people like that try to trip you up. I like to think that he had an inferiority complex and felt threatened by my knowledge. In my dreams.

Endoscopy introduced a procedure called endoscopic ultrasound that required a bit of training in the setup and cleaning of the instruments. I was sent back to Southend on a two-day course in the operation and maintenance of the instruments. I enjoyed that course and learnt a lot about how the system worked. On my return I had to impart my newly acquired knowledge to the rest of the staff. I gave a presentation with graphics showing how it all worked with technical explanations and demonstrations. Naturally if you weren't interested in the technical aspects, it was a bit over the audience's head, so I simplified some of it. I had a go at some procedures whilst on the course such as fine needle aspiration using dummy patients. This is normally performed by a doctor. I also tried ultrasound scanning of live patients. I enjoyed this course although when I booked it and the accommodation I booked to be in a single room. On arrival I was placed in a room with a smoker to my annoyance. I said that I can't have him smoking in the room to which he took his lighter and cigarettes and threw them in bin. I was a bit wary of him as he seemed a bit unhinged. As it happened my stay passed without incident. This was the last course that I attended just before I left endoscopy.

Eventually, I began to feel that the job wasn't going anywhere, I'd reached the point where I couldn't advance any further without retraining completely. The money wasn't great, and I felt that I could do with something a bit more challenging. If they could have offered more money I might have stayed. I wasn't actively looking for another job, but I did keep an eye on the hospital job bulletins. I was at the nurse's station one day casually looking at the jobs posted on the intranet when I clicked on one. The job was for a Trainee Clinical Technologist in Nuclear Medicine. The job was based in Velindre Hospital in Cardiff, a cancer hospital. I didn't think for one minute that I stood a chance of getting the job, but I said to a colleague, "I bet I could do that" to which they replied, "Why don't you then?" I did have some misgivings about my ability to do the job.

I called the number and arranged to go and look around the department. The Nuclear Medicine Department in Velindre was a small department with just six people (at that time). I filled an application and waited not thinking I'd get an interview, but I did.

This was getting serious as they stated that I'd need a scientific qualification to be registered to practice. Luckily, they would pay for me to go to university to gain the necessary qualification. I did doubt my ability to complete a university course, but still carried on. On the day of the interview, I felt calm and ready to answer their questions and if the worst were to happen, I'd still have the job in endoscopy. Once the interview was over, I asked if I could have another look around the department but before that could I have a drink from the jug of squash. I thought I was calm and cool until I held the cup of squash. I had to hold my hand steady with my other hand as I was shaking so much.

I did the tour of the department asking lots of questions particularly about the environmental impact of the radioactivity. I was shown around by Cathy Morgan the Principal Clinical Technologist and eventually I left with them saying they would contact me the next day with a yes or a no.

Back in endoscopy I was going about my business when the

phone rang on the nurse's station. "Fred there's a call for you". It was Ian Davies, the Consultant Physicist in the Nuclear Medicine Department and the lead interviewer at my interview. "We would like to offer you the post" came the disembodied voice. I was shocked and felt a little bit sick. Would I be able to do it? Maths was something of a prerequisite and I am to maths what a dyslexic is to words.

As I accepted the post over the phone, Nicola Lewis who I got on well with was sat at the station listening and burst into tears. I was touched by that. Nicola and I would go into town for tea after work from time to time and I was never quite sure whether she fancied me or not. I played it safe and treated it like a friendship especially as she was sort of going out with a gorilla of a man.

17

So, two thousand and four was my last year in endoscopy, it had been a great time working in that department with many friends being made.

New Year and new job January fourth two thousand and five saw me entering a new era of employment and a profession that required me gaining a science qualification. I was tasked with finding a course that would give me the necessary qualification in a science subject.

A new college was opening in Birmingham "The Mathew Boulton College" that offered the necessary course. I could choose any subject as long as it was science based but I opted for Biomedical Sciences.

The Nuclear Medicine department paid for a train ticket for me to go and see if I could get on the course. Susie came with me so that once I'd finished at the college, we would have a look around the Bullring Shopping Centre.

To get to this college we had to cross what could only be described as wasteland, I had no doubt that this would be built on in the future but there were some unsavoury looking characters dotted about. The college was disorganised, and it was difficult to find someone to talk to about the course. After trying from one place to the next any information wasn't forthcoming so eventually, I gave up and left. I decided that traveling to Birmingham every Thursday and in the winter months walking over the waste land was a bit of a stretch so, with that Susie and I decided that I needed something nearer to home so we enjoyed the rest of the afternoon shopping.

I eventually found a course in Cardiff at the University of Wales Institute, now known as the Cardiff Metropolitan University. I had an interview via phone with the course tutor who accepted me for Biomedical Sciences as a mature student. The course was run every Thursday, so I did day release for three years all paid for by the department.

The post of Trainee Clinical Technologist was an on-the-job training post so my first day was familiarisation and being introduced to practically everyone around the hospital. Jill Jones, the Chief Clinical Technologist took me on a tour of the departments introducing me to all and sundry. I was still unsure whether I had done the right thing but only time would tell. This job was a massive step up from the previous post with the requirement of me being registered to practice and the only way to get registered was to get the science qualification and be employed in the department. During my first year in the job, I was sent on various courses related to working in the hospital such as CPR and the like. It was mostly death by PowerPoint, but I did get sent on a few that were mostly for doctors. I'd be sitting there thinking "What the hell am I doing here?" whilst trying to look interested. Let's face it, I was trying to look like I knew what they were talking about.

As I mentioned earlier, I will now tell you about my time as a mature student at the University of Wales Institute. I really couldn't believe the lack of respect and consideration that the younger students displayed in the three years that I attended. If for whatever reason I was late for a lecture I would enter the lecture room quietly, acknowledge the lecturer then quietly proceed to my place. The number of students that banged open the door, ignored the lecturer and stomped their way to their desk creating as much noise as possible really annoyed me, but the fact that the lecturer just ignored it made it even more incredulous. I suppose they're not allowed to say anything these days in case it upset the student's fragile egos.

I was one of about five or six mature students and all of us were of the same opinion.

I remember one time during a particularly complicated lecture a small group behind us kept talking about nothing in particular and weren't very quiet. As the lecture was on biochemistry it needed full concentration to follow what the lecturer was trying to get across. After this had gone on for a while I'd had enough. I stood up apologised to the lecturer then lambasted the offending crew, telling them that if they wanted to chat and not learn to go outside. They shut up.

There was a short pause as everyone realised that I wouldn't tolerate nonsense, that was followed by a bit of murmuring then the lecturer carried on. There was no more shenanigans and the lecture continued although I still found it difficult to follow. I failed that part's exam, having to resit it. Eventually I scraped through biochemistry, I found anatomy and physiology a bit easier. There was a time when us group of mature students had arrived at a lab a few minutes early for a session. We entered the room and started to don lab coats ready for the lesson. Suddenly a lab assistant came from nowhere shouting at us that we shouldn't be in there and we should wait outside. She was very aggressive, so I decided I wasn't being spoken to like that by a lab assistant. She was raging but I just stared her down saying who does she think she was talking to. We reminded her that we weren't twenty somethings and she only had to say. She stormed off and we went back outside. When the tutor arrived, she asked why we were stood in the corridor, naturally we went to great pains to tell her of our exchange with the lab assistant.

I liked the challenge of this new job and everyone in the Nuclear Medicine department was friendly – bar one. For whatever reason this one person took a dislike to me, and it was a mystery to everyone why. She was literally friendly with the entire hospital; I was the exception. We'd go to break together and she wouldn't speak a word to me.

Eventually I decided I needed to get to the bottom of it, so I asked her if I'd done anything to offend her. I had the response of "It's not you, it's me" so there was no explanation. Things began to escalate, and it was noted that there was a bit of an atmosphere whenever we were working together. As I was new, I didn't want to cause any trouble, so I kept quiet until she started becoming more bizarre in her behaviour. Doing a course that was challenging and having to work in a detrimental atmosphere everyday was starting to get me down. Sue my wife would know if she and I would be working together because I would leave the house quite depressed. There was a complete change in atmosphere when she was away on annual leave and for that time, I would enjoy my work. Unfortunately, things would go back to "normal" upon her return.

I was still in contact with the crew in endoscopy and was often invited to retirements and other events. Sue Barker the sister in charge said after I'd told her about it, that all I had to do was give her a call and they'd have me back. I did consider going back there a few times but decided to stay and see if things improved. They did not and there was one time where it got so bad I nearly walked out and turned my back on Nuclear Medicine altogether. Doing a university course and training on the job while doing battle with this woman was taking a toll on me. I had suffered from irritable bowel syndrome and the stress of this situation was causing a flare up. I called in sick once or twice because it would be me and her working together and I just couldn't face it.

I was working in the lab of the department one afternoon when she came storming in ranting at me about me looking at her emails. I had earlier been in the office and the computer was off until I got up to go to the lab, I bumped the desk which moved the mouse, and the computer came on. She must have left her screen open, and the screensaver kicked in.

After that I was afraid to be left alone with her in case she accused me of something more serious. Behind the scenes unbeknown to me meetings were taking place about how best to proceed with the situation.

The day came when we were sent for mediation. A member of the hospital management sat us down and tried get to the bottom of it. All that happened was her assassinating my character but nearly everything she said was trivial and could have been sorted between us. Nothing changed and if anything, it got worse.

My wife Sue contacted the department to see what was being done about it because she could see the affect it was having on me. Then one day I was walking down the corridor with her slightly ahead of me when she suddenly turned around and rattled off a rail of abuse. It took me by surprise, and I didn't know what to say. I was still trying to settle into the job. I told Ian Davies the Head of the Department what had happened to get my side of the story in first, he said he'd investigate it. I noticed that there was a CCTV camera facing the area where this event happened, so I mentioned it to Ian. I saw him later in the corridor asking somebody from management about the camera. I don't know if they used the footage but soon after things had escalated further and a date for a tribunal was set to take place at the trust headquarters. It turns out that just around the corner from where the event had taken place was someone who'd witnessed it and reported it. I realise that this chapter so far is all about my struggle with being bullied by this woman, but my first three years working in Nuclear Medicine was marred by her total dislike of me.

Anyway, the tribunal took place, and she was given a warning and an opportunity to change her ways. It didn't work and she was taken off the department to work in Radiotherapy in I believe a clerical role. She had trained as a radiotherapist but had moved to Nuclear Medicine many years previously.

In the office, Nuclear Medicine

The pressure was off, and I could avoid her in the corridors or the restaurant, so I was now able to concentrate on my course and training in work. I had a few failed attempts at some of the coursework because I was under so much strain, but I resat them and came through okay.

 Then came the bombshell, radiotherapy didn't want her there, so she was being brought back to Nuclear Medicine. The hospital manager broke the news to myself and Lisa who had also been affected by her attitude to me. My heart sank and I told them that I'd regretted coming there and wished I'd stayed in endoscopy. They persuaded me to give it a couple of weeks, I agreed but, in my mind, I was secretly planning to go back to call Sue Barker and make return to endoscopy.

She came back to the department, but nothing had changed. She still ignored me and had a go if I was a little bit slow or needed more help with something. The atmosphere returned making it awkward for everyone. This went on for a little while longer then, suddenly, she was gone. We think the hospital had paid her off, but we can't be sure. I heard that she had gone on to do a marine biology course and a course like that isn't cheap. I didn't care so long as she was out of my hair.

Eventually, after three years of university and battling with this woman's attitude, I passed my course and was eligible to be placed on the Register of Clinical Technologists and moving up a pay band.

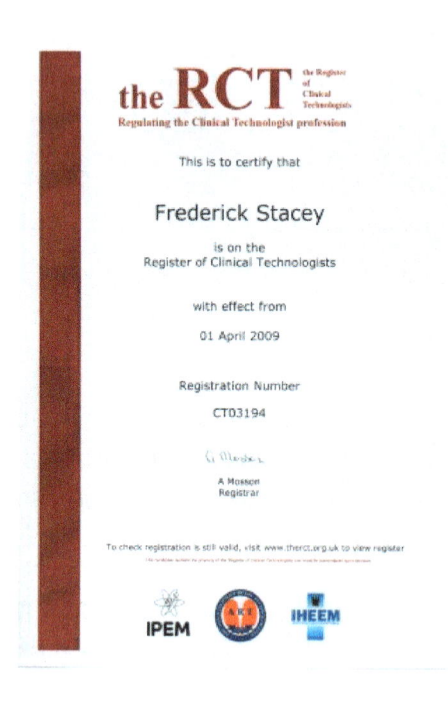

> **the RCT** the Register of Clinical Technologists
> Regulating the Clinical Technologist profession
>
> This is to certify that
>
> **Frederick Stacey**
>
> is on the
> Register of Clinical Technologists
>
> with effect from
>
> 01 April 2009
>
> Registration Number
>
> CT03194
>
> A Mosson
> Registrar
>
> To check registration is still valid, visit www.therct.org.uk to view register
>
> IPEM   IHEEM

I enjoyed working in Nuclear Medicine and got on with everyone in the department and the wider hospital. People would ask me, what happened to so and so, but I would just say I didn't know.

18

The next couple of years I continued gaining more experience in the workings of Nuclear Medicine. Jill Jones, the Chief Technologist and my immediate line manager was also a member of the Salvation Army and got wind of my television and stage exploits and had decided I would be great in one of her plays that they put on every year. At first, I was reluctant as I am in no way religious but after a lot of persuasion, I'd agreed to do at least one.

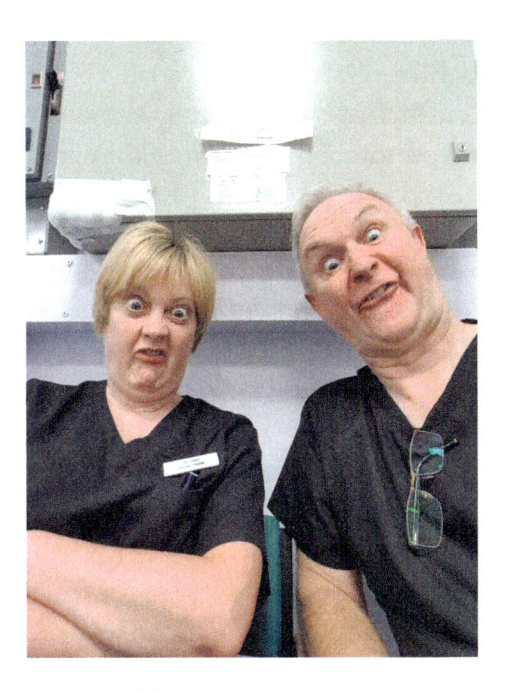

Jill and me

 I Really enjoyed it and got on with everyone there, I went to great pains to tell them that they had a heathen in their midst, but they still welcomed me, and I took part in a few plays and carol concerts over the next few years. Jill also found out that I was a filmmaker so asked if I could help them make a film about Kate Shepherd who'd been sent by William Booth, founder of The Salvation Army to the Rhondda Valleys and founded the first Salvation Army church in the valleys. We made the film over a few months with me using my skills with a green screen. It worked rather well and was well received although given more time and resources think it could have been a bit better. Nonetheless it has been shown a few times in various places and it sold a few copies on DVD, I even got invited by a Women's Institute group to give a talk on the film although I think they thought I was with the Sally army. It was a great experience for all concerned but sadly, a few people who'd taken part are no longer with us. That's life I suppose.

Talking of films, an advert was placed on the hospital's intranet looking for people within Velindre Trust who would like to take part in making a film. Naturally I was first on the phone, well actually an email offering my services. A meeting was called for everyone who'd responded so roles were allocated, and a title was created. I was going to direct "Total Recurl" a film about equality in the workplace. I also ended up playing a nasty patient that I think I played rather well! The film was funded and furnished by Iris in the Community, an LGBTQ+ initiative. I didn't mind that if it meant I was indulging my passion for making films. The film was shot in a day and was and possibly still is used extensively for diversity and equality training within the hospital trust. If you'd like to see the film, it is available on YouTube. Four years later Iris was making another film, this time with a bigger budget and a larger crew, so I put myself forward to direct this one too. "I Shall Be Whiter Than Snow" was based on the true story of a lesbian couple who despite the one partner's terminal cancer diagnosis got married at Velindre Hospital. This film was shown in two cinemas in Cardiff and did a festival run around Europe. Something of a change from my early career in the NHS. When it came to the actual filming, I had retired from the NHS by that time so could spend as much time as I liked working on this film without having to book time off, although I have no doubt they would have allowed me the time to do the filming as they did with the previous one. We filmed this over three days and in various locations around Cardiff.

*

I remember sitting in the hospital restaurant on a break when a man in a very smart suit came in nodding to everyone and saying hello. He took off his jacket and placed it on the back of the chair and went to get a drink. He looked very important, I along with others thought he was a hospital trust bigwig. He continued smiling at people and passing the time of day. He came into the restaurant a few times over a couple of weeks.

On another visit to the restaurant, I asked Wendy one of the assistants if she knew who he was. It turned out that he was a patient from Whitchurch, a psychiatric hospital next door to Velindre. He appeared a few more times until Whitchurch hospital closed. Harmless but wouldn't it have been interesting if he'd sat in on a few meetings. That I would love to have seen.

19

In my later years at Velindre Hospital, a virus was spreading throughout the world and was becoming the most talked about topic around the hospital and beyond. Paul Williams, a colleague had told us that it was going to be global, but we just laughed as the so-called preppers hoarded food and other items for the impending pandemic.

My wife Sue was a health visitor and had caught the virus, although we didn't know it at the time. The following week unbeknown to me I had caught it too and I went into work with what I thought was just a tickly cough. I was sent home after I'd been coughing a lot and was booked to go to one of the testing stations. I was phoned the next morning to say that I had tested positive. I was one of the first people in the hospital to test positive. Because of that we assumed that Sue had been positive too. I was told to stay at home and take paracetamol until I was clear of the infection. As it was the height of summer, we spent a lot of time in the garden. Had it been raining; we would have been couped up indoors.

It was a scary time as there were thousands of deaths from covid countrywide and to say I was worried would be an understatement. Sue did have a serious bought of coughing and vomiting while sweating profusely one day and I was poised ready to call an ambulance, I really thought at that moment I was going to lose her, thankfully it passed, and she got better.

The nation started clapping every Thursday night in support of the NHS and the work they were doing during the pandemic.

Personally, I wasn't sure if it was worth it, but the staff should have been treated better. I was out on the doorstep coughing constantly one evening during the clapping and our neighbours said I looked so ill that they were worried about me. I was my usual stoical self, telling them I was fine!

During lockdown, the entire country had to stay at home unless it was strictly necessary to go out. I eventually shook the virus off and returned to work. As a keyworker I was given a letter to give to give to the authorities if I was stopped on my way to work or on my way home to show them that I was legally allowed out. It was an unprecedented situation.

As a diabetic, I was deemed to be vulnerable, me, vulnerable, I've never been vulnerable in my life but there we have it, I was taken off frontline duties as it was known, so that I wasn't working face to face with patients. I was either in the control room while my colleague attended to the patient in the scan room or in the office booking appointments in both circumstances personal protective equipment (PPE), was used extensively. For one day a week I was seconded to doing identity badges for new staff or replacements for lost badges. After I'd stopped doing that I kept getting asked for new badges for months, eventually everyone cottoned on to the fact that I didn't do that anymore.

I was looking at my Facebook page one evening when I came across a post from Velindre Hospital. A colleague, Donna Campbell had succumbed to covid. I knew Donna and spoke with her almost daily, I was shocked to the core to hear this news. Donna wasn't old probably in her forties, I don't know if she had any underlying health problems, but she seemed fit and well whenever I saw her. It was a sad time in the hospital as she was popular and known by nearly everyone. It was this event that really brought it home to me that I should be taking it a bit more seriously, as I am a person with an underlying health condition and that this pandemic was deadly, and nobody was immune.

When I'd returned to work it was quite surreal as everything had changed, from the way we worked to having to wear a lot of PPE. Patients had to phone to say they were in the car park and were checked to make sure they didn't have any symptoms of covid before they were allowed into the hospital, and they were to be alone unless it was necessary.

I worked in Nuclear Medicine for sixteen years and loved it once the problems I initially had with the other woman had gone. Unfortunately, I had to suffer her for three years before I could feel relaxed and enjoy going to work. I went on to become a Senior Clinical Technologist which required me to dispense radioactive treatments and to give injections. I enjoyed some of the autonmy that the job gave. Dealing with patients some so ill that they didn't have long left.
But I really felt That I was making a difference to their treatment by performing scans and blood tests.
 The hospital was featured in a documentary series of four parts called "Hospital of Hope". I featured in episode four talking to the camera about why we were performing a scan on a patient. The documentary went on to win a BAFTA Cymru award.

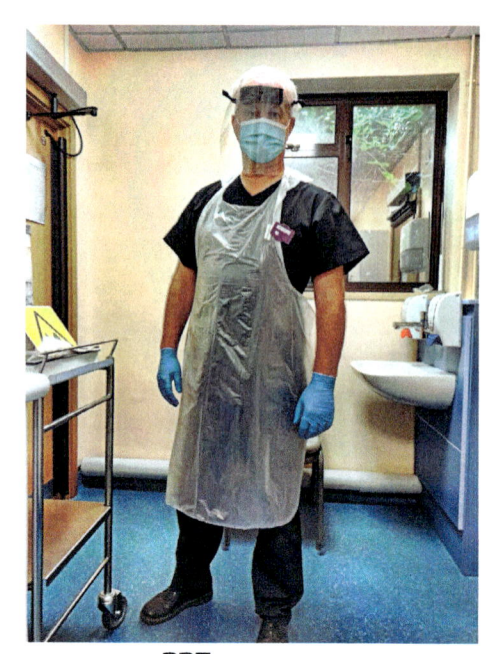

PPE

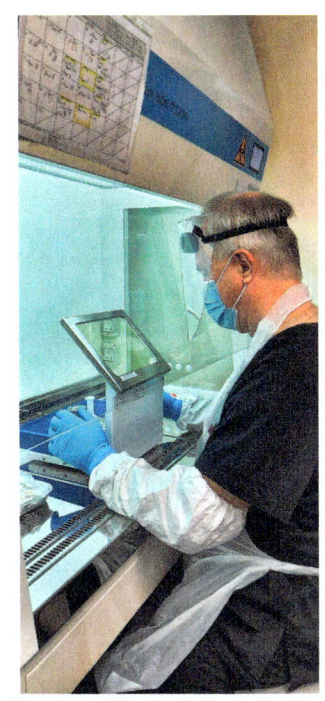

Dispensing Radium injections

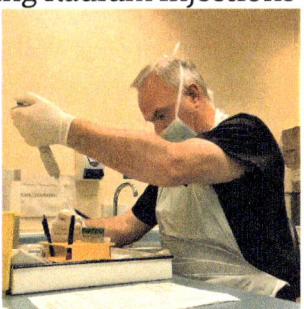

Perfoming a kidney function test

It certainly was a lot more challenging in this role but also enjoyable having the extra responsibility. But after Covid and the close calls with that and the loss of colleagues, I decided I wanted to retire and pursue some of my other interests. So, after a lot of thought and discussion with Susie, I decided it was time to go.

My very last day in the NHS

August the thirty-first twenty-twenty was my last day in the NHS after thirty-eight years' service. I had been a porter, an assistant in Endoscopy eventually becoming a healthcare professional in Nuclear Medicine. I'd finally hung up the uniforms of my NHS career. But none of this would have happened if the Stardust Cabaret Club had stayed open. If I had gone back to work there after it had reopened or if it had never closed, I would have missed the porter's job and my NHS career might never have happened. Sometimes I think fate does intervene.

When people ask what I did for a living I tell them that I worked in the NHS to which they would ask, "Were you a doctor?"

ABOUT THE AUTHOR

Frederick Stacey

Fred worked in the NHS for 38 years first as a porter then finishing as a Senior Clinical Technologist in Nuclear Medicine. In his spare time he volunteers at the local Guildhall. He is also a volunteer speaker for the Commonwealth War Graves Foundation. Fred is a filmmaker and radio presenter. He lives in South Wales with his wife Susie and their dog Alfie and two cats Tigger and Gizmo.

BOOKS BY THIS AUTHOR

Life In The Legion - Marcus And The Romans

My 25 years as a Roman re-enactor depicting our exploits on and off the field, at home in the UK and around Europe.

Printed in Great Britain
by Amazon